AF656335

# INDOMITABLE SPIRIT

Established 1912
100 Years of
Excellence in Publishing
rajpal

₹ 450
ISBN : 9788170288794
I[st] Edition : 2010, 13[th] Edition : 2026
© APJ Abdul Kalam
INDOMITABLE SPIRIT by APJ Abdul Kalam
Printed at Sheetal Prints, Delhi

**RAJPAL & SONS**
1590, Madarsa Road, Kashmere Gate, Delhi-110006
Phone : 011-23869812, 23865483, 23867791
website : www.rajpalpublishing.com
e-mail : sales@rajpalpublishing.com
www.facebook.com/rajpalandsons

# INDOMITABLE SPIRIT

APJ Abdul Kalam

rajpal

# CONTENTS

# INSPIRING LIVES

The basis of all systems, social or political, rests upon the goodness of men. No nation is great or good because parliament enacts this or that, but that its men are great and good[1]

# INSPIRING LIVES

*Everyone's life is a page in the human history irrespective of the position he or she holds or the work he or she performs*

## My Mother

It was a difficult period for our family during the Second World War. I was a ten-year-old boy at the time and war had almost reached our doorstep at Rameswaram. Everything was a rarity and in short supply. Ours was a large joint family with my father and his younger brothers' families all living together, and my grandmother and mother managing this large contingent. At any point of time there would be three cradles at home and the environment alternated between happiness and sadness.

I would get up at four in the morning to go to my teacher Sri Swamiyar for learning mathematics. He was a unique mathematics teacher and would take only five students for free tuition in a year. He had a stiff condition for all his students, which was that they should come to his class at 5 a.m. after bathing. My mother would get up before me, and help me bathe and get ready to go for the tuition. I would come back from the tuition and my father would be waiting to take me for Namaz and to learn the 'Koran Sharif' at the Arabic school. After that I would walk three kilometres to the Rameswaram Road railway station to collect the bundle of newspapers which would be thrown out from the passing Dhanushkodi Mail. I would pick up the newspapers and run around Rameswaram and be the first to distribute them in the town. After that I would return home by 8 and my mother would give me a simple breakfast with a special quota compared to my other brothers and sisters as I was studying and working simultaneously. After school was over, in the evening again I would go around to collect dues from customers.

I still remember an incident which happened those days. All my brothers and sisters and I were sitting and eating and my mother continued giving me chapattis (since we were rice eaters, rice was freely available but wheat was rationed). When I finished eating, my elder brother called me aside and scolded me, "Kalam, do you know what was happening? You went on eating chappatis and mother went on giving you. She has given all her chapattis to you. It is a difficult time. Be a responsible son and do not make your mother starve."

For the first time I had a shivering sensation and I could not control myself. I rushed to my mother and hugged her.

I still remember my mother on a full moon-light night which has been portrayed in the poem 'Mother' in my book 'Wings of Fire':

*I still remember the day when I was ten,*
*Sleeping on your lap to the envy of*
*my elder brothers and sisters.*
*It was full moon night, my world only*
*you knew Mother! My Mother !*
*When at midnight I woke with tears*
*falling on my knee*
*You knew the pain of your child, my Mother.*
*Your caring hands, tenderly removing the pain*
*Your love, your care, your faith gave me strength,*
*To face the world without fear and with His strength.*
*We will meet again on the great Judgment Day*
*My Mother!*

This is the story of my mother who lived for ninety-three years. A woman of love, a woman of kindness and above all a woman of divine nature. My mother performed Namaz five times every day and every time I saw her during Namaz I was inspired and moved.

Womanhood is a beautiful creation of God. I am always inspired and rejuvenated by the memory of two great women, one, my mother and the other, Bharat Ratna M S Subbulakshmi.

**Bharat Ratna M S Subbulakshmi**

Another great mother was M S Subbulakshmi, the mother of Carnatic music. I first heard her in 1950 during the Thiagaraja festival at Tiruvaiyar, which is conducted in January every year. I was studying in college at Trichy at the time and attended this festival with my close friend and music lover Santhanam. After Pancharatna Kriti, M S Subbulakshmi sang the famous Thiagaraja Keertana, *'Endaro Mahaanubhavalu Andhariggi Vandnamulu.'* This song seemed to enter into my being and energise my body and soul with joy and happiness. The meaning was so powerful! I was moved and became a lifetime fan of M S.

> Bhakti *is nothing but the devotion we show to the divinity that resides within us*

According to M S Subbulakshmi, "*Bhakti* is nothing but the devotion we show to the divinity that resides within us. Once we regard the divinity within us with devotional fervour, we are bound to develop the same affection towards everything outside. The reason is that the same divine truth runs through all things. When the devotee has attained this state, service to the world becomes his creed."

I met M S at various music concerts. It was a great joy for me when she was honoured with the Bharat Ratna in 1998 at Ashoka Hall in Rashtrapati Bhawan. I was sitting by her side and she touched my head and blessed me; that was one of the greatest moments in my life. She believed that "Any *raga* has the purpose of directing the mind of the listeners towards God and His manifestations."

When she passed away on December 12, 2004, I was there in her house. Seeing her at eternal spiritual peace, I paid my tribute to her :

*You excelled in Sriragam,*
*And achieved great heights in Bhakti Sangeet.*
*You excelled in the Kirtanas of Annamacharya,*
*Purandaradasa and Trinity of Carnatic music.*
*Even though you may have merged with time,*
*Your music with beautiful deeds*
*Will live for a long time to come.*
*You were born in music, lived with music,*
*And now forever you are merged with divine music.*[2]

**Five Mighty Souls**

Other than my parents and teachers, there are five persons, all of them scientists, who inspired and influenced me and whom I call the 'Mighty Souls'.

## Prof. Vikram Sarabhai

I was fortunate to work with Prof. Vikram Sarabhai for seven years. While working closely with him, I saw the dawn of the vision for India's space programme. It was a one-page statement made in the year 1970 which stated, "India with her mighty scientific knowledge and powerhouse of young should build her own communication, remote-sensing and meteorological spacecraft and launch from her own soil to enrich the Indian life in satellite communication, remote-sensing and meteorology." Witnessing the evolution of this one-page vision into reality through many years of ceaseless work by a cosmic ray physicist and a great scientific mind was a great source of learning for me.

*When I look at Dr Sarabhai's one-page vision statement now and see the results it has created, I am overwhelmed*

When I look at this one-page vision statement now and see the results it has created, I am overwhelmed. Today, we can build any type of satellite launch vehicle, any type of spacecraft and launch it from Indian soil, for which India has all the capability with its mighty facilities and powerful human resources.

## Prof. Satish Dhawan

I learnt a great deal from Prof. Satish Dhawan, a great teacher at the Indian Institute of Science, Bangalore and former Chairman of the Indian Space Research Organisation (ISRO). I worked with Prof. Satish Dhawan for a decade in the development of the first satellite launch vehicle programme for which I was fortunate to have been chosen Project Director.

Prof. Satish Dhawan gave to the country, especially to the young, a great leadership quality which we cannot find in any management book. He taught me a lot through his personal example. The most important lesson I learnt from him was that, when a mission is in progress there will always be some problems or failures, but the failures should not become the master of the programme. The leader has to subjugate the problem, defeat the problem and lead the team to success. This knowledge is embedded in me right from those days and has stood me in good stead throughout my life.

## Prof. Brahm Prakash

Another great teacher who inspired me was Prof. Brahm Prakash. When I was Project Director of SLV-3 programme, Prof. Brahm Prakash was the Director of the Vikram Sarabhai Space Centre (VSSC).

As Director, Prof. Brahm Prakash took hundreds of decisions for the growth of space science and technology. One important decision which I will always cherish was that, once a programme such as SLV-3 was sanctioned, the multiple laboratories and centres of different organisations such as VSSC and ISRO, including the Space Department have to work together as a team to realise the stated goals of the programme. During 1973 to 1980 there was a tremendous financial crunch and there were competing demands from many small projects. But he converged all scientific and technological work to focus on the SLV-3 and its satellite.

Prof. Brahm Prakash is famous for the evolution of management with nobility and I would like to illustrate this with a few instances. He enabled for the first time the evolution of a comprehensive management plan for the SLV-3 programme towards the mission of putting the Rohini satellite in orbit. After my task team prepared the SLV-3 management plan, in a short period of three months, he arranged nearly fifteen brainstorming meetings of the Space Scientific Committee. After discussion and approval, this management plan was signed by Prof. Brahm Prakash and became the guiding spirit and the working document for the entire organisation.

*When a mission is in progress, there will always be some problems or failures, but the failures should not become the master of the programme*

This was also the beginning of converting the national vision into mission mode programmes. During the evolution of the management plan, I could see how multiple views emerged and how people were afraid of losing their individuality due to the main mission, thereby causing much anger and resentment. In the midst of the various management meetings with smoke coming from the cigarettes continuously being lit one after the other, Prof. Brahm Prakash would radiate with a smile, and the anger, fear and prejudice all disappeared in his noble presence.

Today, the space programme, launch vehicle spacecraft, scientific experiments and launch missions all are taking place in the ISRO centres in a cohesive and cooperative manner. I thank this great mighty soul who was a very famous professor in metallurgy at the Indian Institute of Science and evolved the concept of management with nobility.

### Prof. M G K Menon

In a seemingly unconnected or maybe connected way some unique things happened in my life. And two great scientific minds were responsible for making them happen.

In 1962, I was working at the Aeronautical Development Establishment (ADE) in the Ministry of Defence as Senior Scientific Assistant. As the leader of the Hovercraft Development Programme I was responsible for designing, developing and piloting the hovercraft.

One day, my Director told me that a great scientist was coming to ADE, and I must explain to him the design of the hovercraft and also give a flight demonstration. I saw in front of me a young bearded, philosopher-like personality. He was Prof. M G K Menon, the then Director of the Tata Institute of Fundamental Research. My God, how many questions he asked me in twenty minutes! I took him as a co-passenger in the hovercraft, and gave him a beautiful manoeuvred flight on the tarmac. He loved the flight and congratulated me. And I thought that this was the end of it, just like any other VIP visit.

But after a week, I received a telegram (there was no e-mail those days!) asking me to attend an interview for the post of Rocket Engineer at TIFR, Bombay. My ADE Director helped me to get an airlift one way by taking special permission from the headquarters and I went for the interview. Three people were sitting at the interview board; one was Prof. Vikram Sarabhai, whom I was meeting for the first time, the second was Prof. M G K Menon and the third was Shri Saaf from the Administration. What an interview! Prof. Sarabhai asked me questions on what I knew rather than what I didn't know, for me this was a new way of interviewing. Within an hour, after the interview, I was told that I was selected and my life was steered from defence to space programme.

## Dr Raja Ramanna

Another re-entry in my life took place after the completion of the SLV-3 mission. In the year 1981 a lecture series was organised at the Defence Electronics Application Laboratory (DEAL) in Dehradun for a presentation of successful technological and scientific programmes of the nation. Before my presentation, Dr Raja Ramanna, the then Scientific Advisor to the Raksha Mantri gave a talk on Pokhran-I nuclear test and its technological and management challenges. I was the second speaker and Dr Raja Ramanna himself presided.

The topic I dealt with was the evolution of management systems for developing India's first satellite launch vehicle. During lunch time, Dr Raja Ramanna informed me that he wanted me to meet him for ten minutes. I still remember it was at 5 o' clock in the evening, on a Sunday in March 1981. The great nuclear scientist Dr Raja Ramanna told me that he was convinced that I could provide leadership to the missile programme envisaged by the Defence Research and Design Organisation. The focal laboratory for the programme was the Defence Research and Design Laboratory (DRDL) and he invited me to become its Director. I was delighted. That was the beginning of the story of my re-entry into defence leading to evolution of the missile programme, and the rest is history. This 'mighty soul' was Chairman of the Council of the Indian Institute of Science, Bangalore and was responsibile for guiding its destiny for over ten years.

Like all re-entry problems, my re-entry into defence was also a tough job. Even though I was selected by Dr Raja Ramanna, Prof. Satish Dhawan felt that I would not be able to succeed in the environment where I was to work. One person who came to my rescue was a close friend of Prof. Satish Dhawan and the then Director of IISc, Prof. Ramaseshan. I got acquainted with him because of my interest in composite material development. It was Prof. Ramaseshan who persuaded Prof. Dhawan to allow my re-entry into DRDO, without which it would not have taken place.[3]

## Great Visionaries

*Transformation is the outcome of a farsighted vision, innovative mind and guiding spirit*

Foremost amongst some of the visionaries who transformed India by building core competencies in their respective fields using technology and innovative management as a tool was Sri C Subramaniam, a political leader, and an agricultural scientist who, in partnership with Prof. M S Swaminathan brought about the Green Revolution in the '60s. Had the Green Revolution not taken place, we would have continued to have a hand-to-mouth existence in respect of food.

During the same time, Dr Verghese Kurien spearheaded the White Revolution to make India the world's largest producer of milk. Dr Homi Bhabha led research and projects in nuclear energy, resulting in substantial advances in power generation, nuclear medicine and development of nuclear weapons.

## A Visionary can Build a New Nation

President Sheikh Zayed bin Sultan Al Nahayan has been ruler of the Emirate of Abu Dhabi since 1966, and has played a major role in conceiving the federation of the UAE, which was formed in 1971. At that time, the area was just a desert and the camel was the preferred mode of transportation. The Emirate of Abu Dhabi and the other states of UAE were poor and undeveloped with an economy based upon the traditional combination of fishing and pearl-diving along the coast. But due to the invention of the cultured pearl by the Japanese the world market for the Gulf's high quality natural pearls collapsed and the nation could no longer rely on the pearl industry for its economic growth.

But all this is history now and there has been a complete transformation. There are ten-lane roads, modern transportation infrastructure, beautiful flora and fauna, mosques, factories, health centres, schools, swimming pools and a good livelihood for every citizen. This transformation in less than four decades is an outcome of the farsighted vision, innovative mind and guiding spirit of the great personality, President Sheikh Zayed. He transformed the desert into beautiful cities and liveable villages with good telecommunication, transport connectivity, and very high per capita income.

Similarly, the late ruler of Dubai, Sheikh Rashid executed numerous projects for establishing port, air and road connectivity as well as business and trade with a steadfast belief that anything is possible. Dubai's transformation is the result of massive efforts driven by the vision of its rulers.

What made these two great souls of UAE dream and have a vision? The one answer

*She was inspired and motivated be seeing somebody who just goes all out to do something*

that I got was that these visionaries loved their people. They liked to provide a good life to their people through liveable habitat, employment and good environment. For example, water is the most scarce commodity in the desert. But now water is easily available and provided through the process of desalination of seawater. I saw one of the largest desalination plants at Abu Dhabi. In spite of desert conditions, God has blessed them with oil and natural gas and energies drawn from the earth and the sea coast.

These farsighted visionaries utilised the oil and natural gas reserves for the overall development of the UAE and also ensured that the benefits of the new wealth reach out to the people.[4]

## What Inspires You ?

All of us know about Kalpana Chawla, the first Indian woman to go into space. She is a great source of inspiration for all our youngsters. She would say that she is a daughter of the galaxy. She was particularly inspired by the amount of effort put in by her teachers to carry out their courses, the extra time they took to do experiments with the students for coming up with new ideas. She said inspiration came to her every day from people in all walks of life and that she was inspired and motivated by seeing somebody who just goes all out to do something.[5]

# MY TEACHERS

Give me a child for seven years, afterwards, let the God or the devil take the child, they cannot change the child[1]

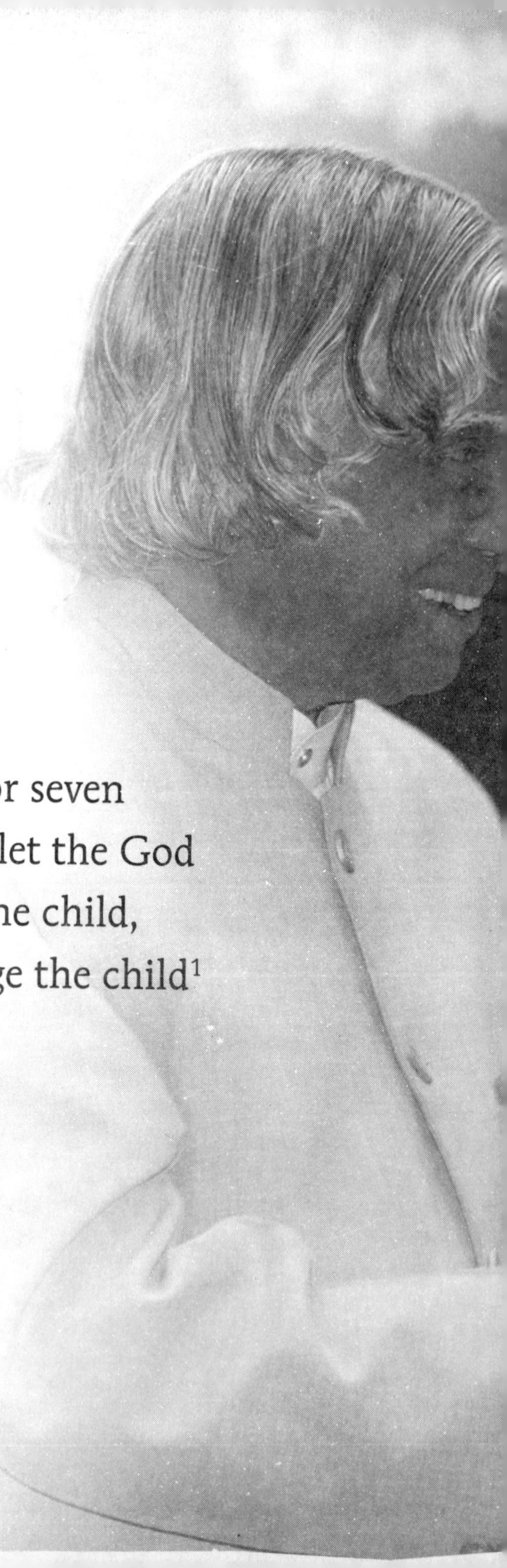

# MY TEACHERS

## Role and Responsibilities of a Teacher

Teachers have a great mission to ignite the minds of the young. The ignited minds of the young are the most powerful resource on the earth, above the earth and under the earth.[2] The role of the teacher is like the proverbial 'ladder'– it is used by everyone to climb up in life – but the ladder itself stays in its place. As in the game of 'snakes and ladders' the ladder can take a person to the world of snakes or to the world of unlimited fortunes. Such is the noble nature of this profession. A teacher's place in our society and in the life of a youngster comes after that of the parents but before God – *matha, pitha guru* and then

*Deyvam* (God). With that kind of recognition, I believe there is no other profession in the world that is more important to society than that of a teacher.[3]

Teachers, particularly school teachers, have tremendous responsibility in shaping the life of an individual. Childhood is the foundation stone upon which stands the whole life structure, as the seeds sown in childhood blossom into the tree of life. And education which is imparted in childhood at the very early stage of development of minds is more important than the education received in college and university.[4]

*I believe there is no other profession in the world that is more important to society than that of a teacher*

The aim of the teacher should be to build character and inculcate values that enhance the learning capacity of children; build confidence to be innovative and creative which in turn will make them competitive to face the future.

The teachers should teach the students the process of learning and enable them to become lifelong autonomous learners and teach them to continuously practise this trait.

Teachers are normally attracted towards the few best performing students and constantly encourage them to succeed further. However, a very important role of a teacher is to facilitate better understanding and learning in those students who are weak in studies. Such a teacher is the real guru.

Let me refer to one of the great leaders of our country, Dr Bhimrao Ambedkar. The significance of Ambedkar's name lies in the full name Bhimrao Ambedkar. Bhimrao was an untouchable student and Ambedkar was his teacher and a high-class Brahmin. Ambedkar took great care of his student Bhimrao, sharing with him not only his knowledge, but often even his lunch. After finishing studies, when Bhimrao became a barrister, in order to remember his teacher, he changed his name to Bhimrao Ambedkar.[5]

*Teachers are the backbone of any country, the pillar upon which all aspirations are converted into realities*

## Qualities of a Teacher

Dr Sarvepalli Radhakrishnan, a great teacher and former President of our country, would give the following advice to teachers: "We must be perpetual seekers of intellectual integrity and universal compassion. These are the two qualities which mark out a true teacher."[6]

A teacher must love teaching and be committed to his profession. Teachers should be lifelong learners. They should not only teach the theory and practical of the subject but they must provide a good grounding on the civilizational heritage and value system of the society. With the use of modern technology, the teachers should groom the students to become autonomous learners.[7]

## Teachers who Influenced Me

In my life my teachers played a very important role. I especially remember two teachers who influenced me greatly and helped shape my life.

## My First Teacher

When I was studying in the fifth class in school at Rameswaram, there used to be a teacher, Sri Siva Subramania Iyer. He was one of the best teachers in our school and all the students loved to attend his class.

One day he gave a lecture on how birds fly. On the blackboard he drew a diagram of a bird, detailing its wings, tail and the body structure with the head. He explained how birds create a 'lift' with the flapping of their wings and use their tail to change direction while flying. For nearly twenty-five minutes he lectured, explaining the various concepts such as lift, drag, and formation flying.

*Learning needs freedom to think and freedom to imagine, and both have to be facilitated by the teacher*

At the end of the class he asked whether we had understood what he had taught. I said that I had not and so did many other students. Sri Iyer did not get upset by our response but instead asked all of us to come to the seashore in the evening.

That evening, the whole class assembled at the seashore of Rameswaram. We enjoyed the roaring sea waves crashing against the sandy hills. Our teacher showed us the sea birds flying in formations of ten or twenty. Seeing these marvellous formations we were all amazed. He showed us the birds and asked us to note what they look like when they fly and the way they flap their wings. He asked us to look closely at the tail and notice how the birds use their tails to fly in the direction they desire.

*A good teacher, with meticulous planning, prepares himself for teaching and the student for acquisition of knowledge*

He then asked us a question, "Where is the engine of the bird and how is it powered?" He explained that the bird is powered by its own life and the motivation of what it wants. All these things were explained to us with a real-life example. Sri Iyer was a great teacher; he could give us a theoretical lesson coupled with practical examples available in nature. This is real teaching!

For me, it was not merely an understanding of how a bird flies. The lesson of a bird's flight created a special feeling in me and I thought to myself that my future course of study would have to be with reference to flying and flight systems. Sri Iyer's teaching and the event that I witnessed helped me decide my future career.

One evening after classes, I asked my teacher, "Sir, please tell me how to progress further in learning all about flight systems." He patiently explained to me that I should complete my eigthth class, and then go to high school, and further on to an engineering college to acquire education in the area of flight systems. If I could complete all my education with excellence, I might do something connected with flight sciences. Following my teacher's advice when I went to college, I studied Physics, and at the Madras Institute of Technology, I opted for Aeronautical Engineering. This advice and the bird flying demonstration provided by my teacher gave me a goal and a mission for my life. It proved to be a turning point in my life which eventually shaped my profession and transformed my life as a rocket engineer, aerospace engineer and technologist.[8]

## My Second Teacher

As an aerospace engineer I worked in Delhi with the Ministry of Defence, and later joined the Defence Development establishment at Bangalore. There, with the advice of the Director, I took up the project for the development of the hovercraft. The design for the hovercraft needed the development of a ducted contra-rotating propeller for creating a smooth flow balancing the torques. Though I knew how to design a conventional propeller I did not know how to design a contra-rotating propeller. Some of my friends suggested that I should approach Prof. Satish Dhawan of the

Indian Institute of Science (IISc) who was well known for his aeronautical research.

I took permission from my director, Dr Mendiratta, and went to meet Prof. Satish Dhawan. He was sitting in a small room filled with books and a blackboard on one wall. Prof. Dhawan asked me what the problem was that I wished to discuss with him. I explained the requirement of my project work and he agreed to teach me the design provided I could attend his classes in the IISc between 2 and 3 p.m. on all Saturdays for the next six weeks. He prepared a list of the reference material and books I should read before attending the classes. I considered this as a great learning opportunity and started regularly attending the classes and meeting Dr Dhawan. Before commencing each meeting, he would ask critical questions to assess my understanding of the subject. For the first time I realised how a good teacher, with meticulous planning, prepares himself for teaching and the student for acquisition of knowledge.

This process continued for the next six weeks, and I understood the integrated concept of designing the contra-rotating propeller. Prof. Dhawan then asked me to design a contra-rotating propeller for a given hovercraft configuration. That was the time I realised that Prof. Satish Dhawan was not only a great teacher but also a fantastic development engineer of aeronautical systems. After completing the design, Prof. Dhawan reviewed it. Then we went for the fabrication of the propeller. Since the special material that was needed was not readily available in the market Prof. Dhawan talked to the chairman of Hindustan Aeronautics Limited who helped procure the material, with which I fabricated the propeller, using multi-layer sandwich construction and assembly.

During the test trials I faced some initial teething troubles. Whenever required Prof. Dhawan would be there to witness the test and help find solutions to the problems. After reaching the smooth test phase, the contra-rotating propeller went through fifty hours of continuous testing. Prof. Dhawan witnessed the test himself and congratulated me. It was a great day for me when I saw the contra-rotating propeller designed by us performing to the mission requirements.

This was the first design I developed and it gave me the confidence to design many complex aerospace systems later in my career. Through this project I not only learnt the techniques of designing the contra-rotating propeller but also learnt how to beat the problems and make the system work in spite of many failures which occur during the development stage.

These two teachers in my life taught me two very important things. One, the teacher provides knowledge and facilitates shaping the student's life with great dreams and aims. Two, the teacher creates self-confidence in the students and helps them inculculate the "I can do it" spirit through the process of education and learning.[9]

Parents and teachers must understand that every one of us on this planet creates a page in human history irrespective of who he or she is. I realise my experience is a small dot in human history, but that dot has a life and light. But a teacher's life lights many lamps.[10]

## A Teacher puts you Decades Ahead

As a young student at St. Joseph's College at Trichirapalli, I had the opportunity of witnessing a scene of a unique divine-looking personality walking through the college campus every morning on his way to teach mathematics to B.Sc. and M.A. students. Young students would look at him with awe and respect. When he walked, knowledge seemed to radiate all around. He was Prof. Totadri Iyengar, the renowned mathematics teacher, a personality symbolising the best of learning and culture.

*Teachers have a great mission to ignite the minds of the young*

At that time, 'Calculus Srinivasan' was my mathematics teacher and he would talk about Prof. Totadri Iyengar with deep respect.

During those days, he and Prof. Totadri Iyengar would take classes for first year students. I had the opportunity to attend Prof. Iyengar's classes, particularly on the subjects of modern algebra, statistics and once I heard him teaching complex variables.
'Calculus Srinivasan' would select the top ten students from his class to the Mathematics Club of St. Joseph's where Prof. Totadri Iyengar would give lectures. I still remember a lecture he gave in 1952 in which he introduced four great mathematicians and astronomers : Aryabhata, Bhaskara, Brahmagupta and Ramanujam. The lecture is still ringing in my ears. Such inspiring learning and lectures became the foundation for my education.

Teaching with value system, my teachers of primary, secondary and college education put me a few decades ahead.[11]

## The Mission of Teaching

The purpose of teaching is to create nation-building capabilities in the students. The capabilities are derived from : knowledge from education, own experience, and value system through civilization heritage. After completing their education the students should have in them, the leadership qualities.

*Teachers should be the best minds in the country*

I visualise enlightened students in hundreds and thousands coming out of each educational campus and enriching the nation and the world towards global peace and prosperity.[12]

There is a statement : "If you have integrity, nothing else matters. If you don't have integrity, nothing else matters." It conveys a very critical message. Flooding the society with 1,00,000 learned students of character and integrity, every five years will indeed bring a big and pleasant shock to the present fragile society. And teachers, who are the gurus, the role models, are the ones who can do this.[13]

### Two-Way Teaching and Learning

*A teacher has to create a lifelong autonomous learner*

Learning needs freedom to think and freedom to imagine. Both have to be facilitated by the teacher and the education system. Teachers have to ask questions which are challenging and allow the students to think and come up with answers. Teachers must also find answers to the questions asked by the students or at least guide the students towards an approach through which they can find an answer. Eventually the teacher has to create a lifelong autonomous learner who will blossom into an enlightened citizen.

During the last five years, I have met over one million students from all parts of the country, particularly in the age group ten to seventeen years, and I make it a point to answer at least ten to fifteen of their questions. In addition, through my website, I have answered thousands of questions of students from India and abroad. I would like to share some of the questions to illustrate the typical curious young minds, particularly to the teachers, so that they should know the expectations, aspirations, intellectual alertness and the dreams of our students.

At the Silver Jubilee function of the Karnataka Rajya Vijnana Parishad attended by children from twelve different schools of Bangalore, some of the children asked very interesting scientific questions. Master Prajwal P. Acharya of ninth standard, Prarthana School, asked, "What is the relationship between time and universal gravitation?" I appreciated this beautiful question and told him that the concept of time, space and universal gravitation is very exciting and has engaged great minds. "Gravity is the force of attraction between massive particles due to their mass. Weight is determined by the mass of an object and its location in a gravitational field. While a great deal is known about the properties of gravity, the ultimate cause of the gravitational force

*The role of the teacher is like the proverbial 'ladder', it is used by everyone to climb up in life, but the ladder itself stays in its place*

remains an open question. General relativity, which postulates a relationship between mass and energy curve, space and time, is the most successful theory of gravitation to date."
The next question came from Master Bharath Choudhari, a tenth standard student from Athena Public School. He asked me, "Why are we not exploring the ocean more than the space?" I told him that the ocean is restricted to the size of the earth whereas space is unlimited. Reaching the depth of the ocean is tougher than reaching heights in the space. In spite of the difficulty in reaching the depth of the ocean, we are exploring it and many benefits are accruing. There are many treasures of knowledge, several interesting forms of marine life and a variety of natural resources being explored from the depth of the ocean.

Another student from the audience asked, "What is the difference between a scientist and a philosopher?" I answered that the thinking process is common to both the philosopher and the scientist. A scientist deals with theory which has to be validated. A philosopher postulates theological, philosophical and spiritual thoughts, the validation of which are the societal dynamics. Science ultimately results in technology and benefits the society. Philosophy leads the way to the dynamics of society.

Teachers should welcome such questions from the students. Particularly between the ages of fourteen and seventeen years, it is very important to infuse in young minds the beauty, challenge and bliss of various subjects. This is the period when students make up their mind whether to pursue science, engineering, medicine, law or humanities.[14]

## Teachers Should be the Best Minds

As a fellow teacher, I can state that teachers are the backbone of any country, the pillar upon which all aspirations of the country are converted into realities. Creativity is the result of the education process and the environment of the school and above all the teacher's capability of igniting the minds of the students. The teacher community is indeed the creator of enlightened citizens.[15] According to Dr Sarvepalli Radhakrishnan, "Teachers should be the best minds in the country."[16]

There are about five million teachers working in our primary and secondary schools. The majority of them are teaching in schools located in the six lakh villages spread all over the country. It is not enough to provide merely the school infrastructure in a village, but there is need to provide an integrated learning environment for the students and an economic environment for the whole family which attracts both the teachers and students to stay on in the village. It is a natural

*A teacher's life lights many lamps*

tendency for the teachers to look for transfers to urban areas since they feel they can educate their children only in big towns or cities. Also they feel that their knowledge can be expanded only with the facilities available in urban areas.

This situation needs immediate attention and we should embark on a massive programme to make the life of these teachers in the villages comfortable and attractive. This can be made possible by providing urban amenities in rural areas through essential connectivities such as physical, electronic, and knowledge connectivity, which in turn will lead to economic prosperity of the villages.[17]

## Technology-Aided Teaching

Our schools, both in urban and rural areas, lack experienced teachers and the per capita availability of teachers is very low. Classes are loaded with forty to sixty children with one teacher and it is impossible for the teacher to pay attention to each student in the available forty-minute period. This results in dilution of quality and non-recognition of creative students, sometimes leading to dropouts.

Technology can assist in overcoming these problems and the gap can be bridged by marrying technology tools and connectivity with quality teachers, which will create and maintain the interest of the students in the learning process.[18]

The model I envisage is the following : Every state can identify certain number of quality teachers of primary and secondary schools. Using these teachers as resource, through tele-education, we can provide quality education to thousands of students instead of forty or fifty students in a normal classroom.

In terms of actual instruction, computers are an invaluable tool for providing active collaborative learning and assessment. While basic word processing programmes allow students to become independent publishers of ideas and opinions, e-mail provides opportunities for peer review and group editing. More sophisticated interactive multimedia packages offer true enquiry based learning, where students can construct and demonstrate solutions in a variety of in-class projects.

*Teachers must be perpetual seekers of intellectual integrity and universal compassion*

This is not to suggest that computers be used to replace or play the role of the teacher. Realistically that would be both undesirable and impractical. Instead, the computer must be recognised as an effective teaching tool which assists the educator. Software offers students individualised learning, so while some students progress in a subject at their own pace, those who begin to fall behind can receive proper personal attention from the teacher. The computer assists the teacher to concentrate on interaction and individualised assistance.

Increased use of tele-education will bring down the cost of operations and simultaneously connectivity (physical, electronic, knowledge and economic) will assist quality teachers teaching in schools.[19]

## Celebrating Teacher's Day

Dr Sarvepalli Radhakrishnan, a teacher and former President of our country, was born on September 5. Whenever people would approach him for celebrating his birthday he would answer that it can be better celebrated as Teacher's Day. That is how September 5 is celebrated as Teacher's Day every year. Being a teacher myself, I always look forward to this important day.[20]

*The purpose of teaching is to create nation building capacities in students*

Parents and students need to participate in the celebration of Teacher's Day and it is essential to celebrate this day in every school in the country. This is the time the school and the parents of the students should recognise the contribution of teachers and celebrate their accomplishments. At this function, selected teachers may be asked to talk about their personal experiences and the methods they follow for creating a unique environment for their students to learn. This type of celebration will motivate other teachers also to perform well in their schools.[21]

Ultimately, education in its real sense is the pursuit of truth with the teacher in the pivotal position who has to continuously replenish and update his knowledge so that his wards will always look up to him as a walking encyclopaedia, as a fountain of love and, most of all, a caring human being. The teacher will look for newer opportunities

to teach latest technological developments and even use them in his classroom so that technology and teacher-assisted learning would be the order of the day in India.

If only the real sense of education could be realised by each individual with the guidance of the teacher, and carried forward in every field of human activity the world will be so much a better place to live in.[22]

# THE MISSION OF EDUCATION

When learning is purposeful,
creativity blossoms,
When creativity blossoms,
thinking emanates,
When thinking emanates,
knowledge is fully lit,
When knowledge is lit,
economy flourishes[1]

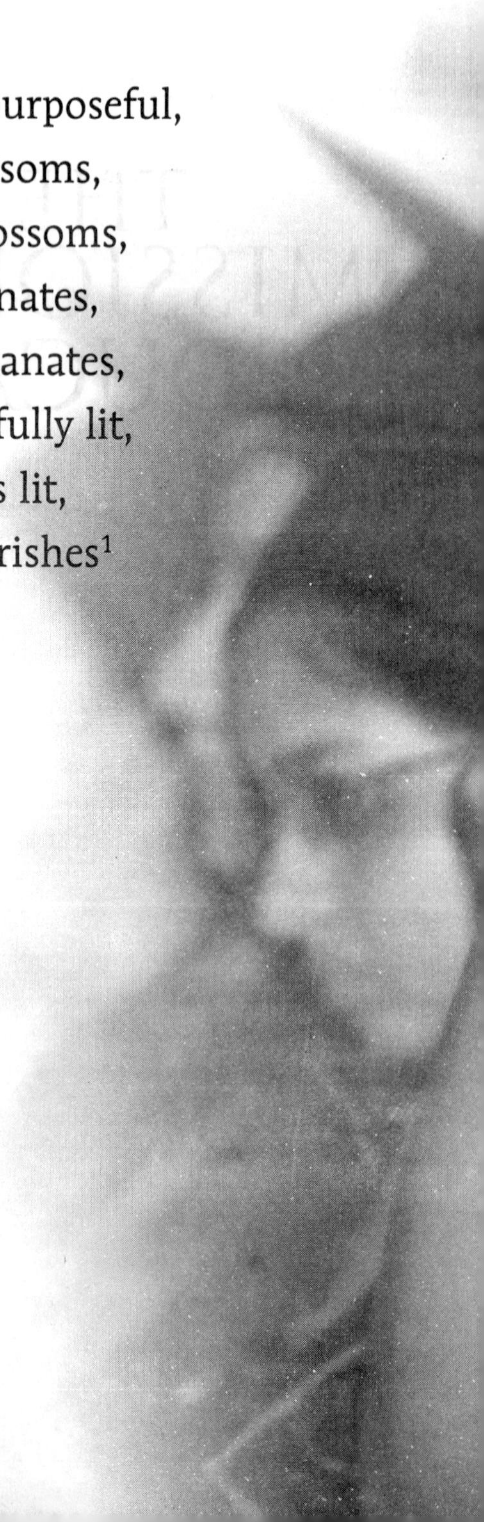

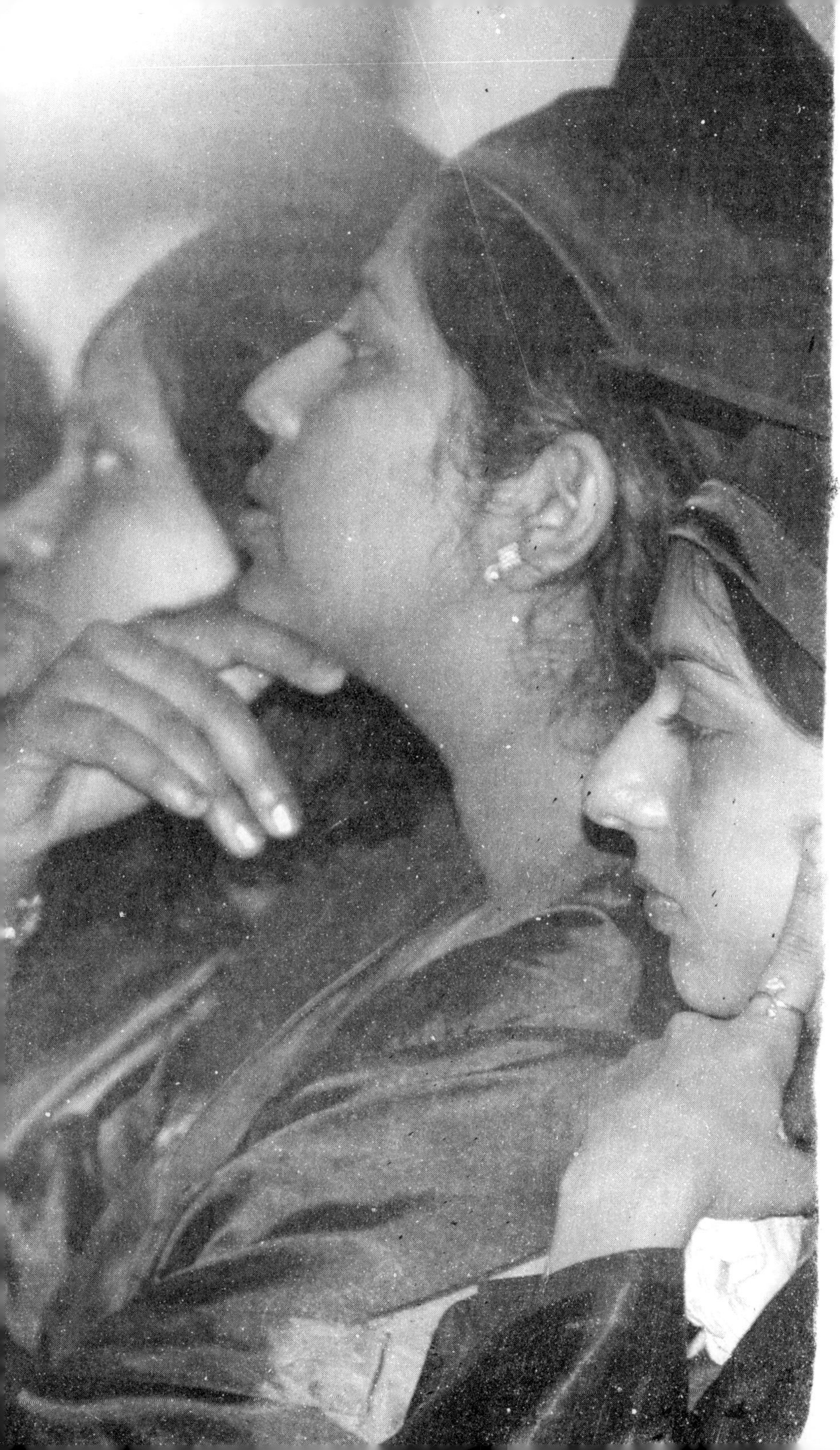

# THE MISSION OF EDUCATION

## Retaining the Smiles of Children

When you look at small children, they are always smiling. When they start going to primary school carrying a big bag on their shoulders, the smile reduces. When they reach secondary school, the smile further reduces and during the higher secondary course, the smile virtually vanishes.

When they enter college they become more serious and after completing college they are in a constant state of worry. During this period the concern of what is next in store for them, inter-linking the financial situation and the competitiveness involved in entering a specific professional field dominates the minds of the children and their parents. This is a situation we all have to strive to overcome.

Can we make an education system which will retain the smiles on the faces of our children throughout the period of their education, right from the time they start attending school till they take up a job? Can we make this possible? This can happen if we make the education system creative throughout, and provide full employment opportunity to all the youth, based on their aptitude and capability.

Creativity in the education system can be promoted by reducing the theoretical burden at the primary level, progressively increasing it at the secondary level, and finally leading to higher level teaching and creation of self-reliance among students to undertake entrepreneurship and be employment generators rather than employment seekers.[2]

*Education is an endless journey through knowledge and enlightenment*

At the primary stage, education must nurture the child's curiosity about the environment and integrate the thinking process with the skills of hand, limb and body. Primary education needs revamping of the syllabus, the teaching methods and the examination system, so that children's creativity is kindled and allowed to grow. Emphasis should be on exploration, innovativeness and creativity through activities. At the secondary stage, emphasis should be on experiments, problem solving and team work.[3]

*Focus of the education system should be to train students to become autonomous learners*

While classroom learning is important, what the child learns by self-observation outside the classroom is equally important. A child must become an active participant in the process of learning through observation, field studies, experiments and discussions. To achieve this, schools must move from being educational centres to becoming knowledge and skill centres.[4]

## The Role of Parents

Parents have an important role in the education of their children and in making them enlightened citizens. They must be aware of the need for good education for the child. Parents should set an example for the child by their overall behaviour and conduct. This will enable the child to develop love and respect for the parents and see them as role models.[5] They should also create an atmosphere for the child to ask questions, elicit answers and freely communicate with them.

## Integrated Mission

For parents and teachers, home and school campus must have an integrated mission as, up to the age of seventeen years, it is the father, the mother and the teacher who play a critical role in leading a child to become an enlightened citizen.

As a child grows up and reaches a school-going age he needs a value-based education which takes place in the school and is an important environment where character gets shaped.

The prime learning period for children is five to seventeen years of age. Students spend approximately 25,000 hours in the school campus during these years. At home, while love and affection are imparted, yet most of the time of the day is spent in doing homework for the next day and studying, eating, playing and sleeping. Hence the school hours for children are the most productive time for learning and this needs the best environment. Schools must provide mission-oriented learning with value system. Twelve years of value-based education in the school campus are essential to establish an open and transparent society. I am reminded of the Greek teacher Bestolozzy's saying, "Give me a child for seven years, afterwards let the God or devil take the child, they cannot change the child." That is the power of a teacher.[6]

## The Role of School

There are a few experimental models of education across the country that are working to promote creativity among children and sustain the student's interest in learning and help reduce the dropout rate.

### Create Willing Learners

Prof. M R Raju lives in his native village Peddamiram close to Bheemavaram, Andhra Pradesh. The life of Prof. Raju is indeed a great example of how a famous nuclear scientist left his job in the USA and came back determined to transform Peddamiram and its surroundings with the support of his family members.

With his own assets Prof. Raju started the Mahatma Gandhi Memorial Medical Trust in the village. In a decade, he and his team, supported by volunteers from various institutions from India and abroad, have brought about a great change in the lives of the people in the village.

He particularly focused on character building and upliftment of children in the age group of three to five years. The village had a hundred children in this age group, out of which fifty belonged to the high income group and studied in private schools; thirty were very poor and studied in a Balawadi School run by the State Government; and the remaining twenty joined the school being run by Prof. M R Raju. In this school the parents pay fee equivalent to half a day's wages per child per month. For girl students they have to pay only ten rupees per month.

The emphasis in this school is on providing a playful environment, nutritional support and caring love. The children are given training in cleanliness and hygiene. For example, they are taught the importance of washing their hands before eating. With this training they become hygiene teachers at home, not allowing any family member to eat food without washing their hands.

*Can we make an education system which will retain the smiles on the faces of our children?*

When the teachers interact with the children they do so in the manner of a scientist. This technique promotes creativity among the children. When a child is shown the letter 'B' and asked what he understands by it, the child says it looks like a spectacle. Similarly, when a sketch is started with some facial feature such as the eyes or lips, the children are able to draw a full picture. This shows the creative ability of the students.

Students, once trained in Prof. Raju's school for three years, learn to enjoy studies and do not become dropouts later. This has totally transformed the village atmosphere and the dropout rate of the children in schools has come down substantially. A confident young population is emerging in the village and the surrounding areas.

This method of training, which is being practised by Prof. Raju and his team for the last ten years, has been researched by child psychologists and educational theorists. This approach makes the child a willing learner before entering the school and makes him participate enthusiastically in the learning process once he joins the regular school. This experiment is being repeated in many other schools.

## Create Lifelong Learners

*Schools must provide mission oriented learning with value system*

In an effort to improve the overall quality of school learning for children, the Azim Premji Foundation, in collaboration with state governments and multilateral agencies, has started a child-friendly school initiative. The principal aim of this programme is to ensure that all children come to school, learn during school time and complete at least five years of schooling. The scheme is effective because of the commitment of the teachers, the village elders and the members of the school committee. The programme encompasses a series of interventions that strengthen practices in the classroom and provide support to educational administration and community empowerment to manage the educational process. The initiative includes setting standards regarding facilities such as classrooms, water, sanitation and services like safety, physical and psycho-social health.

The focus is on gender-sensitive curricula and creating materials for literacy, numeric ability, knowledge, attitudes, skills for life and learning processes.

This holistic phenomenon of learning once ingrained in the primary stage where there is a happy learning process and a non-threatening evaluation has led to voluntary learning by the participants.[7]

## Create Autonomous Learners

In today's world of communication and information, a student has an overload of information coming to him from a multitude of sources. It is possible today for a student to move around with a reasonable-sized library in his laptop computer with access to the entire world of information through the Internet. He no longer needs to tax his brain's storage and recall capacities. The focus of the education system should be to train the students on how to cull the relevant knowledge from this vast ocean of information. The teachers should guide the students in this regard and build a capacity in them to become autonomous learners.[8] Educators must develop a new vision for schools and schooling, a vision of an educational environment in which students can grow more autonomous through the very

*For parents and teachers, home and school campus must have an integrated mission*

act and process of learning. We cannot lecture students into autonomy, rather it must be developed and acquired through a process of action and in the case of schools through the act of learning.[9]

## Recognise and Nurture Talent

Though born in Germany, Albert Einstein as a young student moved to the Zurich Polytechnic Institute in Switzerland to pursue his studies. Entry into the Polytechnic did not require a high school diploma, just a passing grade in its tough entrance examination was sufficient. Einstein failed in the entrance examination but he did exceptionally well in the mathematics and physics sections. This so impressed the Principal that he promised to take in Einstein the following year without an entrance test.

*Education should be imparted with a view to the type of society that we wish to build*

This incident highlights the importance of having a flexible system of admission and the critical ability of a teacher to spot aptitude of a student in a particular subject and nurture the talent.[10]

## The Mission of Education

Every one of us has gone through the various phases of education, from childhood to the time we take up a profession. A scene appears in front of me where there is a child, a teenager, an adult and a leader. All of them are facing a situation of human need, but each one reacts differently.

The child asks, "What can you do for me?" The teenager says, "I want to do it alone." The young person proclaims, "Let us do it together." The leader offers, "What can I do for you?"

The education system has a tremendous responsibility to transform a child into a leader – the transformation from "What can you do for me?" to "What can I do for you?"

This will demand the school or college principal to be a visionary with an inspiring capability. The principal has to ensure that teachers impart learning to the children in such a way as to bring out the best in them and for this he has to be a good teacher himself. The best of creativity among the students will emerge by the integrated influence of principals, teacher, and parents.[11]

*Schools must move from being educational centres to becoming knowledge and skill centres*

According to Dr Sarvepalli Radhakrishnan, "Education should be imparted with a view to the type of society that we wish to build. We are working for a modern democracy built on the values of human dignity and equality. These are only ideals; we should make them living forces."[12]

## An Education Model for the 21st Century

A good educational model is the need of the hour to ensure that students grow to contribute towards the economic growth of the nation.

The entire education system has to be based on capacity building comprising five components : research and enquiry, creativity and innovation, capacity to use high-end technology, entrepreneurship and moral leadership.

*The 21st century is about the management of all the knowledge and information we have generated and the value addition that we can bring to it*

**Research and enquiry:** The 21st century is about the management of all the knowledge and information we have generated and the value addition that we can bring to it. We must give our students the skills with which they can find a way through the sea of knowledge that we have created and continue with lifelong learning. Today, we have the ability, through technology, to really and truly teach ourselves to become lifelong learners which is an important skill required for sustained economic development.

**Creativity and innovation:** The amount of information that we have around us is overwhelming. When information is networked the power and utility of the information grows as squared as predicted by Metcalfe's law. The management of knowledge in the 21st century is beyond the capacity of a single individual and must move out of the realm of the individual and shift into the realm of networked groups. Students must learn how to manage knowledge collectively.

**Capacity to use high-end technology:** All students should learn how to use the latest technologies for aiding their learning process. Universities should equip themselves with adequate computing equipment, laboratory equipment, and Internet facilities and provide an environment for the students to enhance their learning ability. In the midst of all the technological innovations and revolutions we cannot

think that the role of the teachers will be diminished. In fact, the teacher will become even more important and the whole world of education will become teacher assisted as technology would help in tele-porting the best teacher to every nook and corner of the country to propagate knowledge.

*Real education enhances the dignity of a human being and increases his or her self-respect*

**Entrepreneurship:** The aptitude for entrepreneurship should be cultivated right from the beginning and continue all the way up to the university level. We must teach our students to take calculated risks for the sake of larger gain but within the ethos of good business. They should also cultivate a disposition to do things right. This capacity will enable them to take up challenging tasks later in life.

**Moral leadership:** Moral leadership involves two aspects. First, it requires the ability to have compelling and powerful dreams or visions of human betterment. Second, it requires a disposition to do the right things and influence others also to do the right things.

In sum, enquiry, creativity, technology, entrepreneurial and moral leadership are the five capacities required to be built through the education process. If we develop in all our students these five capacities, we will produce 'Autonomous Learners' (self-directed, self-controlled lifelong learners) who will have the capacity to both respect authority and at the same time be capable of questioning it in an appropriate manner. These are the leaders who would work together as 'Self-Organising Networks' with the ability to transform any nation into a prosperous nation.

However, the most important part of education is to inculcate in the students the spirit of 'we can do it.'[13]

## Education must lead to Employment Generation

### Teaching Relevant Skills

While literacy and numeracy are essential for a citizen, these alone are insufficient

to acquire gainful employment. Having the right and economically relevant skills becomes especially critical for those who have education only up to high scbool, and a large percentage of our young people belong to this category. They need to be trained to get into employment or become self employed. They can be taught skills required in construction, repair work, hotel, healthcare industries or in retailing or as electricians, carpenters, etc. The modern competitive economy demands having the required quality skills and it is our duty to empower our citizens with such skills.[14]

*The education system has a tremendous responsibility to transform a child into a leader - the transformation from 'What can you do for me' to 'What can I do for you?'*

## Creating Entrepreneurs

There has been substantial growth in our higher educational system and we are generating around three million graduates every year. However, our employment generation system is not in a position to absorb these graduates passing out from the universities, leading to an increase in the number of educated unemployed. This is also because of a large mismatch between the skills required for the modern economy and the education imparted to most of these students. This situation is bound to lead to instability in the social structure. We need higher education focused on and oriented towards employment opportunities. A multi-pronged strategy is needed to make education more attractive and simultaneously create employment potential. How do we do that?

The educational system should highlight the importance of entrepreneurship and prepare students right from college to be oriented towards setting up of small enterprises and ventures either individually or jointly, which will provide them creativity, freedom and ability to generate wealth. Diversity of skills and perseverance in work make an entrepreneur. These should be taught to all the students.[15]

*The most important part of education is to inculcate in the students the spirit of 'We can do it'*

## What Students Want

Today's young students want the education system to feed and challenge their innovative and creative minds. They are the creators of tomorrow and they want to think about it today. A good system of education should be able to satisfy their insatiable hunger for knowledge.[16]

Educational institutions have to gear up to evolve a curriculum that is sensitive to the social and technological needs of a Developed India. Student activities towards developmental missions should be seamlessly integrated with the existing curriculum so that the future members of the knowledge society are fully developed in all aspects of societal transformation.

Education is an endless journey through knowledge and enlightenment. Such a journey opens up new vistas of development of humanism where there is neither scope nor room for pettiness, disharmony, jealousy, hatred or enmity. It transforms a human being into a wholesome whole, a noble soul and an asset to the universe. Real education enhances the dignity of a human being and increases his or her self-respect and universal brotherhood in its true sense becomes the sheet anchor for such education.[17]

# CREATIVITY AND INNOVATION

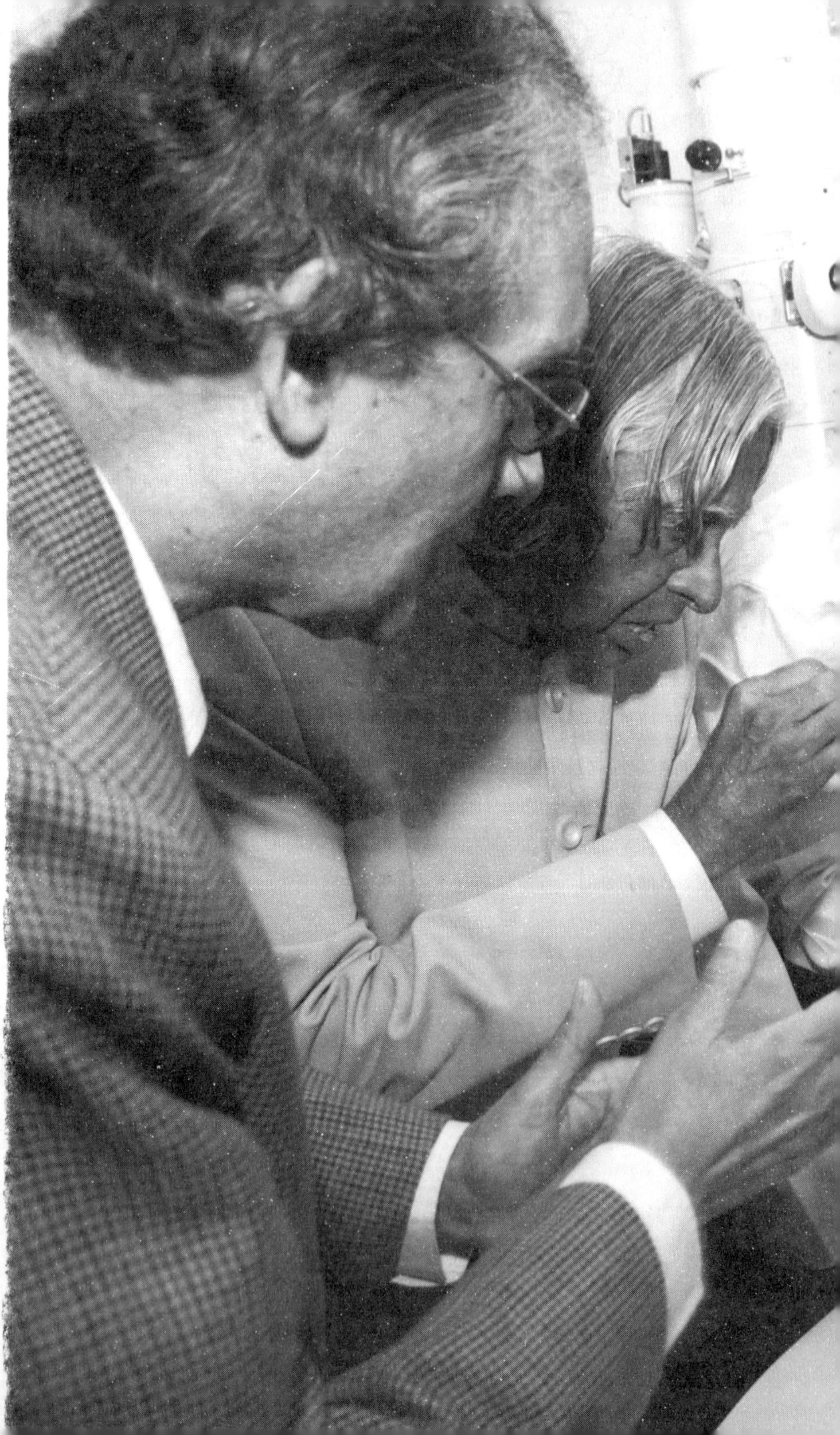

An ignited mind is the most powerful resource on earth, above the earth and under the earth[1]

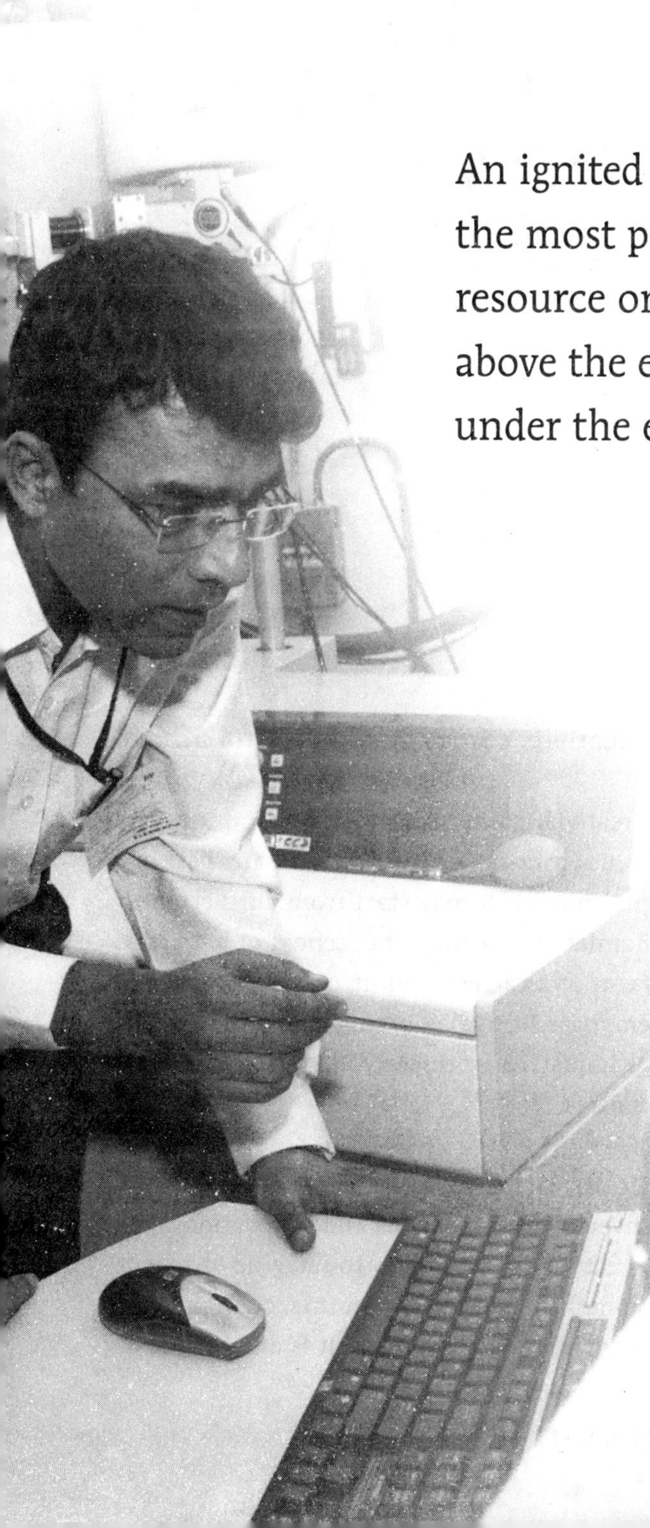

# CREATIVITY AND INNOVATION

## Creativity comes from Beautiful Minds

Creativity comes from beautiful minds. It can come from anywhere and from any part of the country. It may start from a fisherman's hamlet or a farmer's household or a dairy farm or a cattle breeding centre or it may emanate from classrooms or laboratories or industries or research and development centres.

Creativity has many dimensions such as inventions, discoveries and innovations. Creativity is the ability to imagine or invent something new by combining, changing or reapplying existing ideas. It is an attitude to accept change and newness, a willingness to play with ideas and possibilities, a flexibility of outlook, the habit of enjoying the good while looking for ways to improve it. Creativity is a process to work hard and continually improve ideas and solutions by making gradual alterations and refinements. The important aspect of creativity is : seeing the same thing as everybody else, but thinking of something different.

The human mind is a unique gift. Thinking should become our capital asset, no matter whatever ups and downs we come across in our lives. Thinking is progress. Non-thinking is destruction to the individual, organisation and the country. Thinking leads to action. Knowledge without action is useless and irrelevant. Knowledge with action brings prosperity.[2]

*Creativity and imagination of the human mind would always be superior to any computer*

## Promoting Creativity

There is no doubt that there is creativity in every mind but it calls for a concerted effort to ensure that it is expressed. Every mind is creative, every mind is inquisitive, and when children ask questions we must answer them. This is the primary responsibility of the teachers and the parents. If this is done at a young age, creativity will be nourished and children will flourish. This will also promote a culture amongst children to answer the questions when others ask them.

Beautiful minds are the source of creativity. Creativity transforms the thoughts in the form of paintings, stories and poems.

*Learning gives creativity,*
*Creativity leads to thinking*
*Thinking provides knowledge*
*Knowledge makes you great.*[3]

## Nurturing Creativity

*Every mind is creative, every mind is inquisitive*

Loveligen, a young man from a remote area of Kerala, who could not complete his science graduation, wrote to me saying that he had discovered a new mathematical theory and would like to meet me. I saw from the letter that the boy was very sincere. Since he had written to me, I thought our specialist team could study his work and direct him to the right type of researchers. So I called him to Delhi for a few days.

When I saw his work I was surprised to see that he had arrived at part of the equations of Ramanujam's Number Theory, which this boy was not at all aware of. He had discovered something and added some new points to it and the result was new. To a great extent achievements in the field of mathematics generally seem to come out of a desire to look into the beautiful aspects of nature, including natural phenomena such as the star-studded skies, which have always interested astronomers from time immemorial. An additional contributory factor seems to be an inherent drive towards recognition of patterns even if it be in the sense of mathematical sequences or series. It is interesting to note that Loveligen has currently delved into the equally exciting topic of power sequences and series. What I felt was that he needed a good mathematical education and a patronage of a good mathematics teacher. It is like providing a Prof. Hardy for Ramanujam.

How do we promote such young and enthusiastic minds? Can our teachers and philanthropists or the social activists spot these young buds and help them blossom?[4]

## Creativity is Borderless

Shankar's International Childrens' Competition is being conducted every year since 1949. I was going through the Shankar's Childrens' Art Volume no. 55 which is a compilation of paintings made by children from sixty-eight countries. It is amazing to see the great talent they have exhibited in their paintings, poems, stories and articles. While grown-ups start talking about countries and borders, castes and religions, the poor and the rich, the work of the children is seamless and borderless. The children's mind is at its purest form and has no divisive tendencies. The youth of the world indeed provides hope for the future of mankind and I am convinced that the planet earth will be safe in their

*Creativity is seeing the same thing as everybody else, but thinking of something different*

hands. While every one of the works of the children that I had the pleasure of going through will remain fresh in my mind for many years, some deserve special mention.

I was very happy to see the painting made by a German girl Anthea Neums, depicting what the Easter season looks like in the rural environment; the bright colours that she has chosen reminded me of my home town on the seashore, where I spent my childhood days. Fourteen-year-old Supraja Chakravarthy from India narrates a story about the homely middle-class morality and how votes are purchased during an election. It is clear that the young mind wants a change.

Thirteen-year-old Aardhra Krishna has worn her thinking cap and let her imagination fly. She has visualised what the earth would look like in 3000 A.D. In her imagination, the citizens are forced to migrate to Mars and make it their home, setting up a flourishing civilisation. This advanced man-made civilisation suddenly faces a threat of extinction created by nature in the form of an asteroid of Jupiter coming towards Mars. The scientists on Mars come up with a very innovative plan of a barrage of nuclear cannons to attack the oncoming asteroid. The bombardment destroys the asteroid and the year 3000 sees a Martian civilisation surviving the fury of nature. What creative scientific thinking of Aardhra Krishna!

*Beautiful minds are the source of creativity*

A poem, 'Never Think of Illness' written by twelve-year-old Anna Sinyakova from Russia amazed me. I always believe that there will be some problem or the other while doing important tasks, but problems should not become the master. My advice particularly to the young children is that you should defeat the problem and succeed. The same thoughts are echoed by Anna Sinyakova. She sends out a very strong message of encouragement and advice through her poem that one must have the courage to face any disease to keep up the spirit of well-being.

*The whole universe is friendly to us and conspires to give the best to those who dream and work*

The way Savidhya Kumari Premasundera, a ten-year-old girl from Sri Lanka, has imagined the scene of fishing and fishermen is testimony to the alertness and the observation capability of the young mind. A thirteen-year-old boy recounts his personal experience of his maiden flight which was hijacked. The entire incident had been so deeply engraved in his young mind and he has been very eloquent in bringing out his experiences and emotions in his writing.[5]

## Creativity Changes Life Patterns

Charles Darwin, who propounded the theory of Natural Selection, made us think differently about the evolution of the human race. Thomas Alva Edison, who invented electricity revolutionised every field of science and technology. Mahatma Gandhi, who started the *ahimsa dharma* movement against racial discrimination in South Africa, fought against British rule and wrested freedom for India through non-violence. These three significant events of the 20th century are the results of creative minds.

*With determined efforts you can always succeed against established beliefs*

Look at the sky and you will see we are not alone. The whole universe is friendly to us and conspires to give the best to those who dream and work. Like Chandrasekhar Subramaniam who discovered the Black Hole; today, using Chandrasekhar's limit we can calculate for how long the sun will shine. Like Sir C V Raman who looked at the sea and questioned why the sea should be blue and which led to the birth of the Raman Effect. Like Albert Einstein, armed with the complexity of the universe, asked questions about nature of the universe, and arrived at the famous equation $E=mc^2$. When $E=mc^2$ is in the hands of noble souls we get electricity using nuclear materials, in an extreme situation the same equation can be used to develop weapons of mass destruction.

In ancient days, Ptolemaic astronomy was a widely used system in calculating the dynamics of various stars and planets. The assumption at the time was that the earth is flat. What a scientific struggle had to take place to prove that the earth is spherical in shape orbiting around the sun. The three great astronomers, Copernicus, Galileo and

Kepler gave a new dimension to the world of astronomy. Today, we take it for granted that the Earth is a globe orbiting around the sun and that the sun orbits in the Milky Way. All the technological advancements we have today are the outcome of scientific and creative explorations of scientists of earlier centuries.[6]

## Creativity can make the Impossible Possible

What we have seen in science and technology in the last sixty years has proved that what was thought impossible has happened and what is thought possible has not yet happened but it certainly will happen. Particularly in the field of aeronautics, space technology, electronics, materials, computer science and software products, the world has progressed to new dimensions. In the coming decades, we may see the birth of unified field theory integrating gravitational forces, electro magnetic forces and general relativity theory, space and time as functions. Young people may also see in their time the establishment of habitat or industry on one of our planets or moon by the human race. The world may also launch solar power satellites through reusable launch vehicle (hyper plane) system for electricity needs, as fossil-based fuel would become rare in fifty to hundred years. All these are possible only through creative minds.[7]

*It is through the process of innovation that knowledge is converted into wealth*

According to the laws of aerodynamics, the shape of the bumble bee is such that it should be impossible for it to fly. But the bee's determination to fly is strong and it keeps fluttering its wings and these high frequency vibrations create a vortex which enables it to fly. With determined efforts you can always succeed against established beliefs. That is the power of creativity.

*The national innovative capacity is a country's critical potential to reinforce both its political and economic entity*

Not only was the bumble bee's flight, but even human flight was considered impossible. In 1890, the well-known scientist, Lord Kelvin, who was the President of the Royal Society of London, said that anything heavier than air cannot fly. But two decades after that, the determination of the Wright brothers made the impossible possible and proved that man could fly. Their success is a story of how sheer perseverance and creativity leads to success. This singular achievement gave birth to the transport revolution and has made the world a smaller place.

Von Braun, the famous rocket designer who built the Saturn-V to launch the capsule with astronauts and made the moon walk a reality once said, "If I am authorised, I will remove the word impossible from the dictionary."[8]

## Creative Indians

In India many innovations and creative thinking took place at various phases of our development.

In the 1960s, none of us dreamt that nuclear energy can lead to electric power generation or that nuclear medicine would one day be used for the treatment of thyroid disorder and cancer. Homi Bhaba's vision led to electric energy generated by nuclear power flowing into grid and within another decade it may increase to more than 20,000 megawatts of power.

In the 1980s, India had a very low base in Information Technology (IT). Some young entrepreneurs, with their innovative and

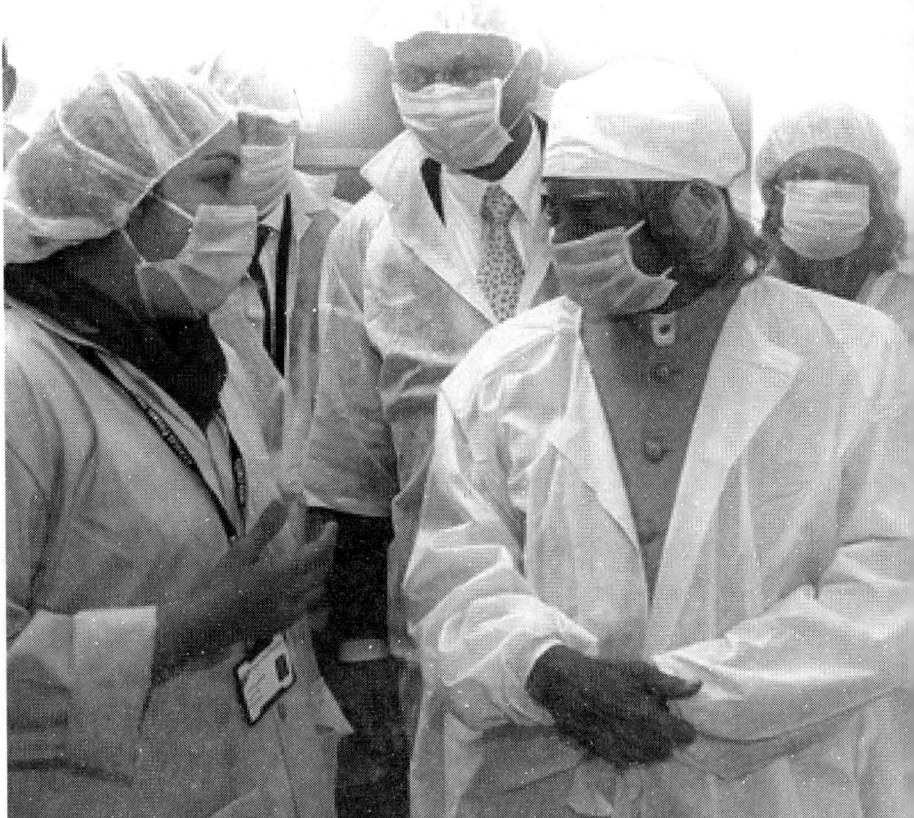

creative thoughts, within the difficult boundary conditions of India's rules and regulations, showed how IT-enabled services can fetch export revenue. Seeing this success the government introduced innovative and liberalised IT policies. Now, our young IT entrepreneurs are earning an export revenue of billions of dollars. Similarly, the pharma industry is making a positive impact on the Indian economy.[9]

## Future Developments

According to Ray Kurzweil, the author of the famous book 'The Age of the Spiritual Machines', the 1000-dollar computer in 2009 will perform trillion calculations per second; in 2019, a million trillion calculations per second, equalling the power of the human brain. By 2029 it will have the power of a thousand human brains! Hence the human beings in future can offload some of their functions to the computer-based robotics and make use of their brain to effectively beat the computer through human innovation and imagination capabilities.

By the end of this century there would be a strong trend towards merger of human thinking with the world of machine intelligence that the human species initially created. When there would no longer be any clear distinction between human anatomical brain and computers, how are we going to retain the supremacy of human being over machines? Computers are going to give us a challenge. It is a question not only for the biologists and bio-technologists, but for the entire scientific community, which would have the great responsibility of keeping mankind above the man-made computers. Fortunately, the creativity and imagination components of the human mind would always be superior and would subjugate the machines. The human genome is full of software that is yet to be fully activated to unleash the ingenious potential of the human species.[10]

*In the new digital economy information that is circulated creates innovations and contributes to national wealth*

## Creativity leads to Innovation and Wealth

Information that is static does not grow. In the new digital economy information that is circulated creates new innovations and contributes to national wealth.

It is through the process of innovation that knowledge is converted into wealth. Innovation is a systematic, organised, rational work usually done in many stages like analysis, tests and experiments.[11]

Innovation needs courage :

*Courage to think different,*
*Courage to invent,*
*Courage to discover the impossible,*
*Courage to combat the problems and succeed.*[12]

Innovation is usually market driven. Innovation can mean bringing about a marked improvement in the performance of a product or system by adopting alternative technologies or bringing about cost reduction by using the most cost-effective methods. An innovative product makes a leap in the benefits-to-costs ratio in some areas of endeavour. What we see in optical communications is speed vs cost. In flexible manufacturing systems it is choice vs cost. In the web-enabled processes, it is customer satisfaction vs cost.

Innovation tends to emanate from research and development as well as from other sources, including organisational change. Hence, there is an urgent need to establish an efficient innovation system in the country. Such a system would involve creation of clusters, which are networks of interdependent firms, knowledge-producing institutions (universities, colleges, research institutes, technology providing firms), bridging institutions (e.g. think tanks, providers of technical or consultancy services) and customers linked in a value-addition creating production chain. Thus, an innovative system with its clusters would tap the growing stock of global knowledge, assimilate and adapt it to local needs and finally create new knowledge and technology.

The national innovative capacity is a country's critical potential to reinforce both its political and economic entity with commercially relevant competitive products in the global market place. This capacity is distinct from purely scientific or technical achievements and focuses on the economic application of new technology. Thus, for building innovative capacity, we require the partnership of private sector, public sector, and academia as a group.[13]

## The Foundation of Human Thinking

Creativity is the foundation of human thinking and will always be at the highest end of the value chain irrespective of the growth of computers with respect to speed and memory. Creativity will continue to be the forte of humankind and enormous computing power provided by technology would be the effective tool that the human mind will use to craft its plans to create a better world to live in.[14]

# ART AND LITERATURE

Art is a benign expression of the inner beauty in nature. Be it a cartoon, sculpture or literary composition, it elevates the beautiful spirit of life for everyone to see and enjoy. Such a spirit silently but eloquently conveys the message of love, humour, affection and peace...[1]

# ART AND LITERATURE

## Art Helps Life to Survive

Our planet Earth has witnessed the birth of many great human civilisations at different periods of time, but only a few of them managed to survive. The ones that did were those which had the capacity to see the future and the ability to adapt to the dynamics of change. This ability is the function of the thinking capacity created by literature, poetry and, other dialectical inputs. Ancient philosophers, and in later years, scientists, technologists, economists and sociologists, all in unison, enriched the various human civilisations. Our Indian civilisation accepted and absorbed the dynamic changes of multicultural impact. That is how we have a society of a billion people of multi-cultures, multi-languages and multi-religions with unity of mind. Thanks to our thinkers, we see the tradition-producing epics such as 'Mahabharata' and classics like 'Thirukkural', 'Kabirvani' and 'Narayaneeyam' continuing to survive and flourish over the centuries.[2]

*Art helps to bring out the beauty of life in its noblest forms, imparting meaning and depth to human existence, justifying and vindicating the purpose for which life was evolved*

## Books–Our Eternal Companions

Coming into contact with a good book and possessing it is an everlasting enrichment of life. A good book becomes a permanent companion. Sometimes, books are born before us, they guide us during our life journey and continue to do so for many generations.

At the age of twelve, Albert Einstein experienced a wonder in the form of a little book on Euclidean plain geometry given to him by his mentor Max Talmud. Through this book Einstein came into contact with the realm and concept of pure thought and learnt how to explore universal truths, without any expensive laboratories or equipment, limited only by the power of the mind.

## My Favourite Books

The most commonly asked questions during my interaction with the youth are:

Which are your favourite books? Which book are you currently reading?

*It is the privilege of authors that they can help mankind endure adversities and succeed in life*

Though I cherish reading almost all books, there are three that I have enjoyed the most. One is 'Light From Many Lamps' edited by Lillian Eichler Watson. I had bought this book in 1953 from an old bookstore in Moore Market, Chennai, and it has been my close friend and companion for more than five decades. It has been so much used that it has had to be bound and re-bound many times. Whenever I face a problem, I turn to this book and it helps wipe away my tears. When happiness overwhelms me, the book again softly touches the mind and brings about a balanced thinking. I realised the importance of the book again, when a friend of mine who is in the judiciary recently presented me with a new edition of the same book. He told me that the best thing he could give me was this book. Maybe fifty years from now the same book may take a new *avatar!*

The second book which I venerate is Thiruvalluvar's 'Thirukkural'. It provides an excellent code of conduct for life, and the author's thinking which extends beyond the narrow concept of a nation, language, religion, and culture indeed elevates the human mind.

The third book is 'Man the Unknown' by Dr Alexis Carrel, a doctor turned philosopher and a Nobel laureate. This book highlights how, in an ailment, both the mind and the body need to be treated as the two are integrated. You cannot treat one and ignore the other. In particular, children who dream of becoming doctors should read this book. They will learn that the human body is not a mechanical system; it is an intelligent and integrated organism made of psychological and physiological systems with an intricate and sensitive feedback system.[3]

*Books were always my friends*
*Last more than fifty years*
*Books gave me dreams*
*Dreams resulted in missions*
*Books helped me confidently take up the missions*
*Books gave me courage at the time of failures*
*Good books were for me angels*
*Touch my heart gently at the time*
*Hence I ask young friends to have books as friends*
*Books are your good friends.*[4]

## The Importance of Authors

Authors of books play a very important role in human life. A good book from an author is a source of great knowledge and wealth for many generations. Sometimes a book may not inspire readers during the author's lifetime but the importance of the book's message becomes more clear with the passage of time when its value is realised by society. Then the book starts shining. Of course, there are some classics which shine continuously for many generations.[5]

*Authors act as conscience keepers of the society*

Jayakanthan, the Tamil author bestowed with the 38th Jnanpith award says, "Going past you (reader) is my (author's) success." Providing a route for the reader to traverse and go beyond himself or herself is a measure of literature's success.

*Give one hour a day exclusively for book reading and you will become a knowledge centre in a few years*

I cherish Jayakanthan's view of life as explained in the introduction to one of his collections of essays titled *'Oru Ilakkiyavadhiyan Arasial Anubavangal'*, which means, 'A Literary Person's Political Experiences' in which he says : "Has not the time arrived for our freedom fighters and socialist thinkers with knowledge and courage to get together and sacrifice to create a new independent society? When will that time come? The literary mind has a passionate longing for it." This is similar, in a small way, to a situation in which Jayakanthan says : "In my writing in literature, even if I am made an outcaste, I will continue to work in the realm of literature, looking for change, as it happened with Jagath Guru Adi Sankaracharya, accepting Dattatreya as Guru. It is not my wish, but it is God's will."

What a beautiful and moving statement. When I read this statement, tears welled up in my eyes because, though I see despair and fatalism all around, faith is challenging them. That is how literature elevates the mind and authors act as conscience keepers of the society.

The galaxy of our thinkers and writers can facilitate the creation of enlightened leaders amongst our youth. Through their writings, they can inspire our younger generation on the capacity for greatness of heart and spirit of mankind and remind them of the need for indomitable spirit with which they can conquer any signs of weakness and despair. This is not a duty cast on the authors, but it is their privilege that they can help mankind endure adversities and succeed in life.

A country is rich because of the natural wealth, biodiversity and its people. But the crowning glory of the nation is its thinkers, who lead the society ahead of its time, and make society accept the change.[6]

Children and students should be encouraged to follow the advice, "Give one hour a day exclusively for book reading, you will become a knowledge centre in a few years." People should make it a habit to give books as gifts especially to the youth. These actions will enrich our youth and assist them in transforming our society into a knowledge society.[7]

## Music, Dance and Drama

We have a rich civilisational heritage of more than five thousand years blending literature,

music, dance and drama. The experience of seeing the artists perform makes me wonder whether music and dance can be used as instruments for ensuring global peace and act as a binding force. In recent years, terrorism has taken a heavy toll of many innocent lives. Is there any alternative solution other than the military, economic and judicial approach to end this problem? I am convinced that music and dance can be one of the important tools for containing terrorism.

Music and dance elevate you to a different plane altogether and give you a breeze of happiness and peace. Music and dance can emanate only when the artists themselves are at peace and in a happy state of mind. In this state they become an elegant example of propagators of peace and happiness.[8]

Music unites. And what better proof do we need than Carnatic music! Its trinity sang their *kritis* in Telugu and Sanskrit in Tanjore district; Purandaradasa sang in Kannada, Annamacharya in Telegu and Arunagirinathar in Tamil. But for music lovers, the language never mattered. Music establishments at Travancore in Kerala, Tirupati in Andhra Pradesh, Thanjavur in Tamil Nadu and Mysore in Karnataka — all of them dazzled like gems in a necklace. The thread of music united these beads. Music itself is a great communication and language can never be a barrier.[9]

*Music and dance can be used as an instrument for ensuring global peace and act as a binding force*

Uday Shankar, who is regarded as the father of modern dance in India, gave an altogether new and wholesome definition to Indian dance and music. He was able to appreciate the wonderful variety and scope of expression afforded by different classical and folk dance forms of our country and incorporate them into a unique artistic expression resulting in an enriched dance vocabulary of the highest level of excellence. A veritable pioneer of renaissance in Indian arts during the 1930s and 1940s, he was instrumental in introducing Indian dance forms and music to the Western world, earning for them worldwide acclaim, respect and admiration. That Uday Shankar did not have any formal training in any of the schools of classical dance and yet could carve a niche for himself in the world of art is eloquent testimony to the fact that he was a born genius.[10]

During my visits to different parts of the country I saw that the rural folk and the tribal communities nurture great love for music and dance. Many a time they just need the slightest opportunity to break into song and dance. This helps not only in smoothening out the rough edges of their tough countryside life but also in preserving, propagating and developing our age-old cultural traditions. The evolution of our music, dance and theatre has been woven by the rural folk into the very history of our nation. The intermingling of diverse streams which make up our composite culture has fully enriched our tradition of artistic expression and should be actively encouraged.[11]

Drama has been a great form of entertainment for invigorating the minds of people. It can be a powerful medium for delivering messages and planting imaginative ideas and thoughts. This form of art has been under great pressure due to cinema, TV and multimedia, which have their own role. But we need to recapture many of our ancient drama forms, and the rich traditional stories embedded in them.[12]

## The Power of Films

People from the film industry have the ability to make the audience laugh, make them cry, and even make them angry, inspire them and at times also depress them. They can touch the emotions of the viewer and create an impression in his mind temporarily or at times even for a long period. Such is the power of a film.[13]

*The crowning glory of a nation is its thinkers*

## Art Elevates the Spirits

Recently, I happened to study a book called 'Articulations—Voices from the Contemporary Indian Visual Art.' I was searching through the book to find out what is the unique quality of the great community of visual art and painting. What is their medium? What is the relationship between the society and the artists? Is there any connectivity between the medium of the artist, such as ink and brush, and society?

When M F Hussain says paintings are the output of the society, it means : if the society is a mediocre society, you will get mediocre paintings, if the society is intellectual and prosperous, the paintings will reflect the situation. Going through 'Articulations', I realised that every painter and artist is a unique personality in search of beauty out of every event which enriches him. While R K Laxman loves to paint crows as they stand out against any background, K K Hebber is inspired by the rhythmic movement of lines. I tend to agree with one of the artists who says that the artists should have 'partnership with the known, the unknown will express itself.'

*Music is a great communication and language can never be a barrier*

Sometime back I composed a poem titled 'Life Tree' in Tamil and translated it into English. The message in the poem was about celebration of life. While composing it I never thought that a poem could be given visual life, beauty and creativity. Around that time a young artist called Manav came and stayed at Rashtrapati Bhawan to picturise the natural beauty of the Mughal Gardens. He stayed with his family for two weeks and created beautiful canvases bubbling with life. I could see in his paintings the beauty of the flowers, smell the fragrance of the flowers, and taste the honey in the flowers. When he came across my poem 'Life Tree' he fell in love with it and spent seven days in the beautiful environment of the Mughal Gardens transforming 'Life Tree' into a speaking tree.

*Every painter and artist is a unique personality in search of beauty out of every event which enriches him*

What a beautiful creation! For the first time I realised how painting and poetry intertwine in the imagination of a painter, leading to the birth of a new creation. That new creation touches your heart, soothes your feelings and transmits beauty and peace of the combined art into every artistic person and showers happiness in his or her mind and soul.[14]

## Prosperity and Art

The prosperity of any nation depends directly on the creativity of its artists and writers. You would remember from your history lessons the fact that during the golden period of any empire there was always a large number of artists and writers supported by the kings and courts.

Students of art and literature are important contributors to transforming India into a developed nation. They will find ample job opportunities in the arena of creative entertainment and management which are the areas where future society would be spending enormous amounts of time and money. They can also act as an effective interface between the people and the policy makers as well as between the people and the scientists and technologists.[15]

Art is a benign expression of the innate beauty in nature. Be it a cartoon, sculpture or literary composition, it elevates the beautiful spirit of life for everyone to see and enjoy. Such a spirit silently but eloquently conveys the message of love, humour, affection and peace.

Art helps to bring out the beauty of life in its noblest forms and takes it on to a higher, better and more civilised plane, imparting meaning and depth to human existence, justifying and vindicating the purpose for which life was evolved. What more can you ask for, what more can you look for in a strife-stricken world where eternal human values are being mercilessly trampled upon and the beauty of life lost in relentless materialistic pursuits.[16]

# ABIDING VALUES

See the flower, how generously it distributes perfume and honey. It gives to all, gives freely of its love and, when its work is done, it falls away quietly. Try to be like the flower, unassuming despite all its qualities[1]

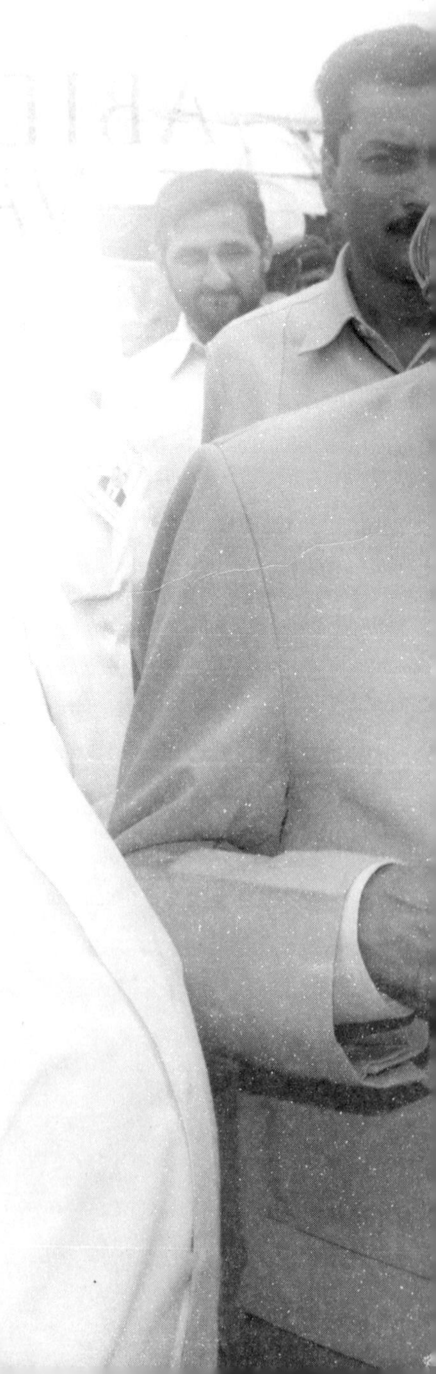

# ABIDING VALUES

## Righteousness

There is a beautiful song emanating from Prasanthi Nilayam, which advocates global peace through the development of righteousness :

*Where there is righteousness in the heart,*
*There is beauty in the character.*
*When there is beauty in the character,*
*There is harmony in the home.*
*When there is harmony in the home,*
*There is order in the nation.*
*When there is order in the nation,*
*There is peace in the world.*

We can see a beautiful connectivity of heart, character, nation and the world. How to inject righteousness in the human heart? This indeed is the purpose of human creation.[2]

We are going through a complex situation as many of us are completely at war with ourselves, with society and with the world. At every instant there is a war in our mind, whether we should go in one direction or another. Whenever there is a dilemma, we must seek wisdom from the Almighty to lead us to the path of righteousness.[3]

In a society we have to build righteousness among all its constituents. For the society as a whole to be righteous we need creation of righteousness in family, righteousness in education, righteousness in service, righteousness in career, righteousness in business and industry, righteousness in civil administration, righteousness in politics, righteousness in government, righteousness in law and order, and righteousness in justice.[4]

*The right kind of education on moral values will upgrade the society and the country*

## Righteous Homes

If a country is to be corruption free and become a nation of beautiful minds, the three key societal members who can make a difference are father, mother and teacher.

One of the staff members of the Indian Institute of Science at Bangalore shared with me this incident. He said that he had taught his daughter that she should always speak the truth and that if she were to do so she would have nothing to fear in life. Today she is ten years old but when she was in the second standard, once she had missed school for a day because she had gone with her father to a function at his friend's place. In her leave letter the father wrote that due to unavoidable circumstances his daughter couldn't attend school. She immediately remarked, "Why should I say unavoidable circumstances and not that we had to attend a function? You have taught me not to tell lies. Why should I tell lies?" The father immediately realised his mistake and re-wrote the leave letter giving the true reason for his daughter's absence.

*From the emperor down to the common man, the cultivation of the righteous life is the foundation for all*

This is the power of teaching children at a young age to be honest, which also enables us to be corrected by the child if we deviate from our righteous path. Honesty comes out of righteousness. Once taught, the children become conscience keepers. Once you start giving the right direction to the minds of the children, character building emanates within the family. "I will make my home a righteous home" should be the motto of each and every child and every parent.[5]

During one of my interactions with students, a student from Shimoga in Karnataka asked me the following question : "What role can students play to stop corruption which is so deeply rooted in our country like cancer?" The agony of the young mind is reflected in this question. For me it was an important question since it comes from a young mind. I said there are one billion people in the country and nearly 200 million homes. In general there are good citizens everywhere. However, if we find that people in a few million homes are not transparent and not amenable to the laws of the country, this is what we can do : These homes, apart from parents, have one daughter or one son or both. If the parents in these homes are deviating from the transparent path the children can use the tool of love and affection and correct the parents to come back to the right path.

I asked all the children assembled in the gathering that, in case parents of a few children deviate from transparency, would they boldly tell their parents that they are not doing the right thing. Most of the children spontaneously responded, "We will do it." This confidence comes because they have love as a tool.

Similarly, I have asked the parents the same question at several other meetings. Initially there is a silence, but later, many of them hesitantly agree that they would abide by the childrens' suggestion since it is driven by love. They also take an oath that "I will lead an honest life, free from all corruption and will set an example for others to adopt a transparent way of life."[6]

## Mother gives the Principle of Truth

Sheikh Abdul Qadir Al-Gelani was a great saint who lived in Afghanistan about one thousand years ago. One day when child Abdul Qadir was grazing his cows, he heard a cow saying, "What are you doing here in the grazing fields? It is not for this that you have been created." He promptly ran back to his house feeling utterly terrified and climbed on to the roof of his house. From there he saw a large group of people returning from the Arafat Mountain, after performing Haj. Bewildered, Abdul Qadir went to his mother and asked her permission to make a journey to Baghdad to pursue a career in knowledge. His mother heard the divine call and promptly gave permission to Abdul Qadir to go. She gave him forty gold coins, which was his share of inheritance from his father, and stitched them inside the lining of his coat. When she stepped out of the door to bid him farewell, she said, "Oh, my son! You are going! I have detached myself from you for the sake of

Allah knowing that I shall not see your face again until the day of the last judgment. But take one advice from your mother : Always feel the truth, speak the truth and propagate the truth even when your life is at stake."

Abdul Qadir set out with a small caravan heading for Baghdad. While passing through rough terrain a group of robbers on horses suddenly attacked the caravan and started looting. None of them however took the slightest notice of Abdul Qadir, until one of the looters turned to him and said, "You here! Poor beggar! Do you have anything with you?" Abdul Qadir replied, "I have got forty dinars which are stitched by my mother in the lining of my coat underneath my armpit." The looter smiled and thought that Abdul Qadir was just joking and left him alone and moved elsewhere. A second looter came and asked the same thing. Abdul Qadir again repeated his answer. This looter also didn't believe him and left him. When their leader came they took Abdul Qadir to their leader and said to him, "This boy looks like a beggar but claims that he is in possession of forty gold coins. We have looted everybody but we have not touched him because we don't believe that he has got gold coins with him and is trying to fool us." The leader put the same question to Abdul Qadir who gave the same reply. The leader ripped open his coat and discovered that indeed Abdul Qadir had forty gold coins inside the lining of his coat. The astonished

*The three key societal members who can make a difference are father, mother and teacher*

leader asked Abdul Qadir what prompted him to make this confession. Abdul Qadir replied, "My mother made me promise always to be truthful even at the cost of my life. Here, it was a matter of only forty dinars. I promised her and shall never betray her trust, so I told the truth."

The looters started weeping and said, "You have adhered to the advice of your great mother but we have been betraying the trust of our parents and the covenant of our Creator for many years. From now onwards, you shall become our leader in our repentance." And they all decided to give up robbing and looting and become righteous persons. This is how the world saw the birth of a great saint, Sheikh Abdul Qadir Al-Gelani, starting from a truth a mother gave to her child.[7]

*Once taught the children become conscience keepers*

## Imparting Moral Values

After every child is nurtured during the early years with love and affection and when he reaches a school-going age he needs a value-based education. The prime learning period for a child is from six to seventeen years of age. Hence, the school hours for children are the best time for learning, and they need the best environment and mission-oriented learning with a value-based educational system.

While I was studying at St. Joseph's College at Trichy, I remember the lectures given by Rev. Father Rector Kalathil. Every Monday, he would take class for an hour talking about great spiritual, religious and political leaders, present and past, and the qualities that make for a good human being. In this class he would give lectures on personalities such as Buddha, Confucius, St. Augustine, Califa Omar, Mahatma Gandhi, Einstein, Abraham Lincoln including some scientific personalities, and moral stories linked to our civilisational heritage. I am convinced that what I learnt in that class of moral science stands by me even today.

It is essential that schools and colleges arrange a lecture by a great teacher of the institution once a week for one hour on India's civilisational heritage. This class can be called a Moral Science class. This will elevate the young minds to love the country, to love other human beings and elevate the young to higher planes.

*Conscience is the divine light of the soul*

The right kind of education on moral values will upgrade the society and the country.[8]

## Gift extinguishes the Dignity of Human Life

Rameswaram is a beautiful island and I lived there as a young boy with my family. It was around 1940, and the Second World War was in progress when the Rameswaram Panchayat

Board elections took place and my father was elected as a member; and the very same day he was also elected as president of the Board. My father was elected as the president not because he belonged to a particular religion or a particular caste or because he spoke a particular language or for his economic status, but only on the basis of his being a good human being. I was a school boy at that time studying in the fourth class and I still remember an incident that took place the day my father was elected.

*Conscience is a great ledger where our offences are booked and registered*

Those days we did not have electricity and I would study with the light of a kerosene lamp. I used to learn by reading out aloud and was reading my lessons loudly when I heard a knock at the door. People never locked their doors in Rameswaram at the time. Somebody opened the door and came in and asked for my father. I told him that father had gone for evening Namaz. He said, "I have brought something for him, can I keep it here?" Since my father was not home, I shouted for my mother to get her permission. But as she had also gone for Namaz there was no response. So I asked the person to leave the items on the cot, and I went back to my lessons.

I was reading aloud and fully concentrating on my studies when my father came back and saw a *tambalum* kept on the cot. He asked me, "What is this? Who has given it?" I told him somebody came and left it for him. He opened the cover of the *tambalum* and saw the costly dhoti, *angawastram*, some fruits and sweets and the slip of paper that the person had left behind. I was the youngest son of my father and he really loved me. But this was the first time I ever saw him get so angry and it was also the first time that I got a beating from him. I got frightened and started crying. My mother rushed and embraced me and started consoling me. Seeing me cry my father touched my shoulder lovingly with affection and advised me never to receive any gift without his permission and explained that receiving a gift with a purpose is a very dangerous thing in life. He quoted a verse from Hadith which means, 'Gifts accompany poisonous intentions.' This experience taught me a valuable lesson for life which is deeply embedded in my mind even today.

Writings in 'Manu Smriti' warn all individuals against accepting gifts given with a motive since it places the acceptor under an obligation to the person who gives the gift. Ultimately it results in making a person do things which are not permitted by law in order to favour the person who has given the gift. Therefore it is necessary that the quality of not yielding to the attraction of gifts and presents must be inculcated in individuals, so that they may develop immunity against the desire for receiving gifts. It is also said that by accepting gifts the divine light in a person gets extinguished.[9]

*Corruption is an assault on the conscience*

## Cultivate Your Conscience

Conscience is the divine light of the soul that burns within the chambers of our psychological heart. It is as real as life is. It raises its voice in protest whenever anything is thought of or done which is contrary to righteousness.

Conscience is a form of truth that has been transferred through our genetic stock in the form of knowledge of our own acts and our feeling of right or wrong.

*What matters in this life more than winning for ourselves is helping others win*

Conscience is also a great ledger where our offences are booked and registered. It is a terrible witness. It threatens, promises, rewards and punishes, keeping all under its control. If conscience stings once, it is an admonition; if twice, it is a condemnation.

Cowardice asks, 'Is it safe?'
Greed asks, 'Is there any gain in it?'
Vanity asks, 'Can I become great?'
Lust asks, 'Is there pleasure in it?'
But Conscience asks, 'Is it right?'
Why have we become deaf to the voice of our conscience? Insensitive to its pricks? Callous to its criticism? The answer is corruption.

Corruption is an assault on the conscience. The habit of taking bribes and seeking favours has become very common. People holding important positions have developed inconsiderateness towards their conscience. They pretend that everything is all right. Do they not know of the law of action and reaction? Have they forgotten how impressions of the subconscious mind and its forces work? If you take bribes, your thoughts and actions are registered in the subconscious mind. Will you not be carrying forward your dishonesty to the next generation and causing them great suffering?

It is a painful reality that corruption has become a way of life affecting all aspects of our life, personal as well as social. It is not merely the pecuniary corruption but its other forms as well. Immoral ways of people holding high positions and handling power have taken the feeling of guilt out of the minds of lesser mortals. What a dangerous situation!

A virtuous man alone can use the instrument of conscience. He alone can hear the inner voice of the soul clearly. In a wicked man this faculty is dead. The sensitive nature of his conscience has been destroyed by sin or corruption. Hence he is unable to discriminate right from wrong. Those who are leading organisations, business enterprises, institutions and governments should develop this virtue or the ability to use their own conscience. This wisdom of using a clean conscience will enable them to enjoy freedom from anxiety and all kinds of worries.

If you do wrong actions and sinful deeds and treat them lightly today, you will not hesitate to perform serious crimes tomorrow. If you allow one sin to enter and dwell in your conscience, you certainly pave the way for the entry of a thousand sins. Your conscience will become blunt and lose its sensitivity. The habit of doing evil deeds will pervade the whole body like the poison of a scorpion.

Do you know when you are corrupt, your children, who are enjoying the fruits of your corruption, are mocking you? After all, they are well informed and knowledgeable. Your parental mask is too thin to hide the contempt of your children. You are no more the role model of your own children. Is this not disgrace enough?

Our society is fast reaching a stage where the conscience of people holding positions of consequence is being challenged by corruption, just as HIV challenges the body's immunity of an AIDS patient. Corruption has seeped into every stream of our lifeblood. Can we save ourselves as a civilisation?

Spiritual leaders have evolved morals, codes and teachings of righteousness. Many beautiful hymns, songs and prayers have been written and composed but the annihilation of conscience by corruption appears frightening. Religion has not been effective in evoking our conscience. Who then will? Can our conscience be redeemed?[10]

## Noble Thoughts

Once, as I was leaving for Bangalore for a lecture, I spoke to a friend and told him that I would be talking to young people and asked if he had any suggestions. He did not give any suggestion as such but offered me the following words of wisdom :

> When you speak, speak the truth; perform what you promise; discharge your trust. Withhold your hands from striking, and from taking that which is unlawful and bad.
>
> What actions are most excellent? To gladden the heart of a human being, to feed the hungry, to help the afflicted, to lighten the sorrow of the sorrowful and to remove the wrongs of the injured.
>
> All God's creatures are His family; and he is the most beloved of God who tries to do most good to God's creatures.

*Think ever of rising higher, let it be your only thought*

He told me that these are the sayings of Prophet Mohammed. My friend who told me this is a great-grandson of the Deekshidar of Tamil Nadu and is a *Gnanapathigal* (Vedic scholar). Such an outlook is possible only in our country where many of our enlightened citizens go beyond their own religion and appreciate other religions also.[11]

There is a beautiful couplet or *kural* in 'Thirukkural' by the peot-saint Thiruvalluvar written 2200 years ago :

*Ulluvathellam uyarvullal matratu*
*Tallinum tellamai nirttu*

It means think ever of rising higher. Let it be your only thought. Even if your object be not attained, the thought itself will have raised you.[12]

### A Noble Action

*A candle loses nothing by lighting another candle*

At a sports meet for the physically and mentally handicapped children conducted by the National Institute for the Mentally Handicapped, Hyderabad, I witnessed an unforgettable incident. In one race, nine contestants, all physically or mentally disabled, assembled at the starting line for a 100-metre race. At the starting signal, they all started out, not exactly in a dash, but with a relish to run the race to the finish and win. But one little boy stumbled on the asphalt, tumbled over a couple of times, and began to cry. The other eight heard the boy cry. They slowed down and looked back. And then they all turned around and went back, every one of them. One girl with Down's syndrome bent down and kissed him and said, "This will make it better." Then all nine linked their arms together and walked together till they reached the finish line. Everyone in the stadium stood and clapped and the cheering went on for several minutes.

People who were there that day are still telling the story. Why? Because deep down we know this one thing : what matters in this life more than winning for ourselves is helping others win, even if it means slowing down and changing our course. I would say that you do not have to slow down. Rather by helping others through the difficult areas, the feedback will make you go faster. If you pass this on, we may be able to change our hearts as well as someone else's. A candle loses nothing by lighting another candle.[13]

## The Path of Righteousness

Righteousness of the heart of the human being leads to a perfect life of an enlightened citizen. This is beautifully explained by the Chinese philosopher, Confucius, in the ascent and descent phase of human life wherein he states :

"People who desire to have a clear moral harmony in the world would first order their national life; those who desire to order their national life would first regulate their home life; those who desire to regulate their home life would first cultivate their personal life; those who desire to cultivate their personal life and set their heart to righteousness would first make their wills sincere; those who desire to make their wills sincere would first arrive at understanding; understanding comes from the exploration of knowledge of things. When the knowledge of things is gained, then understanding is reached; when understanding is reached, then the will is sincere; when the will is sincere then the heart is righteous; when the heart is righteous then the personal life is cultivated; when the personal life is cultivated, then the home life is regulated; when the home life is regulated, then the national life is orderly; when the national life is orderly then the world is at peace. From the emperor down to the common man, the cultivation of the righteous life is the foundation for all."[14]

*Our righteous toil is our guiding light,*
*If we work hard, we all can prosper.*
*Nurture great thoughts, rise up in actions,*
*May righteous methods be our guide.*[15]

# SCIENCE AND SPIRITUALITY

Science is the best boon that God has bestowed upon mankind. Science with reasoning becomes the capital of society... The convergence of science and technology with spirituality is touted to be the future for both science and technology, and spirituality[1]

# SCIENCE AND SPIRITUALITY

### Science is the Best Boon

It is said that the God Almighty wanted to create the best creation. He worked for millions of years, designing and evolving the image. He went on looking at the image, improving it and finally decided to give it life. As soon as the image of the man got life, two things happened. First, he opened his eyes and smiled. God was very happy. The second, he opened his mouth and said, "Almighty, thank you." God was delighted to see His creation and felt that he did the two right things.

Suddenly, God found that something was missing in the man. He then created fire in

a flash of a second, out of which came the *Shaitan*, who said, "God, you took millions of years to create the man, but you created me out of fire in a flash of a second. So, I am the best." The Almighty, who had created the universe with mighty orbiting galaxies with orbiting stars and planets was bewildered with the outburst of *Shaitan*. He had created the best of his creation, the man on one side, and on the other side, the *Shaitan*. He thought of it and looked at both with benevolence and integrated the man and *Shaitan* and gave the following message :
"I have created the human being with brain and thinking faculty. I command all My creations to use your faculty with reasoning to reach My image."

As Rumi, the Turkish Sufi poet, wrote :

*Angel is free because of his knowledge,*
*The beast because of his ignorance,*
*Between the two remains the son of man to struggle.*

*Science and spiritualism seek the same divine blessings for doing good for the people*

This is the mission of human life and science is the best boon God has bestowed upon mankind. Science with reasoning becomes the capital of the society. In whatever field we work, be it science, technology, medicine, politics, policing, theology, religion or judiciary, we have to remain in the service of the common man whose well-being is central to all human knowledge and endeavour.[2]

## Science is Universal

Science is all about asking questions and finding the right answers through hard work and research into laws of nature. Keep asking questions till you get satisfactory answers. Only questioning minds have made the world a liveable place in spite of the world's non-linear dynamics.[3]

*Science tries to provide solutions for a better material life, while spiritualism looks at answers on how to lead a righteous life*

Science is a fascinating subject. And for a scientist it is a life-time mission. Mastery in science needs understanding of mathematics. Mathematics, in combination with science, shines. What is needed is confronting theory with experimentation.

Students get attracted to science if there are scientific problems which trigger their curiosity, are practically relevant, and are beautiful to pursue. The teachers must be role models in the world of knowledge and worthy of emulation in day-to-day life. Creating an education system that has all the above ingredients is solely in the hands of the teachers and educationists. The solution is universal and does not depend on the country you live in because science and scientific pursuits are borderless.[4]

With the advances in information technology, the world has shrunk and become a global village and networking of scientists is necessary to solve the complex real world problems. In ancient times, India was a preferred destination for learning and research in science and philosophy. But in the past few decades the scientist movement in India has been from the East to the West. Of late, we have again started seeing the trend of visits by scientists from the developed nations to India. This is because of the recognition of the calibre of the Indian scientists and some of the state-of-the-art facilities that we have created.[5]

## Science in Pre-Independence India

*In whatever field we work, we have to remain in the service of the common man whose well being is central to all human knowledge and endeavour*

In India, science and technology has had a two-phase progress, the first being the momentum created in the 1930s by the great scientists of international repute who gave the country a new confidence. We remember the pioneering contributions to science made by Chandrasekhar Subramaniam for his Chandrasekhar Limit and Black Hole, Sir C V Raman for his discovery of the 'Raman effect', Srinivasa Ramanujan for his contribution towards the number theory, J C Bose in the area of microwaves, S N Bose, famous for Bose-Einstein statistics and Meghnad Saha for 'Thermo-Ionization Equation'. This phase can be considered the glorious phase of Indian science and the scientific foundation laid by these scientists triggered the later generations.

The one unique similarity in all these scientists was that they had dedicated their entire life to the cause of scientific research and the spirit of inquiry in their chosen field despite all the hurdles and problems in their life. It is a question of dedication, commitment and understanding and also a question of providing a conducive environment for research in science, which gives birth to a true scientist.[6]

## Importance of Science Today

*Science is all about asking questions and finding the right answers through hard work and research into laws of nature*

At the time of our independence, the country was infested with various problems and there was need to urgently bring in technologies for steel, civil structures, hydro dams and thermal power stations. Our concentration was directed towards solving burning problems such as feeding the population, providing water, shelter and healthcare. The political visionaries at that time, in spite of our having a very weak economy, had the indomitable spirit to decide wisely to set up what ultimately has become the science base of our country : centres of research into atomic energy and space. The country also set up a powerful educational base with the creation of the Indian Institutes of Technology and many universities with a unique blend of science and technology.

Today, India has become one of the strongest in the world in terms of scientific manpower capability and maturity. We are in a position not only to understand the technologies that we may have to borrow, but also to create our own technologies with extensive scientific inputs of indigenous origin. In many areas such as pharma, we are delivering to the world products which are backed by large amount of research and development.

We have come a long way since our independence, from being mere buyers of technology to making science and technology an important contributor to national development and societal transformation. In a world where the power of a country is determined by its share of the world's knowledge as reflected by patents and research papers, it is important for India to get its act together to become a continuous innovator and creator of science and technology-intensive products. The science that we work with today must have the innovativeness and the foresight and the vision for it to be the centre of the technology that we develop tomorrow for the competitive world.[7]

## Science and Technology Interface

Technology has various dimensions. One leads to economic prosperity and another creates the capability for national security. For example, developments in chemical engineering which created fertilisers also led to creation of chemical weapons. Likewise, rocket technology, developed for atmospheric research, led to launching satellites for remote—sensing and communication applications also led to the development of missiles with specific defence needs that provide security for the nation. Computer science and mathematics, coupled with communication technology, led to the birth of information technology. Using the same information technology, various fields of administration, commerce, health and education have been transformed into e-governance, e-commerce, tele-medicine, and tele-education.[8]

Technology is the non-linear tool available to humanity which can effect fundamental changes in the ground rules of economic competitiveness. Science is linked to technology through application. Technology is linked to economy and environment through manufacture. Economy and environment linked to technology promote prosperity in the society.[9]

## Self-Reliance in Critical Technologies

For the first vision of our nation, namely, political independence, the leaders and the people worked for the freedom and we achieved it. Now we have before us the second vision of realising a 'Developed India by 2020'.

This vision has five missions, namely, agriculture and food processing; education and healthcare; information and communication technology; infrastructure development including power; and self-reliance in critical technologies. India can be developed only if it has all-round economic prosperity and self-reliance in critical technologies. Therefore, it is essential that the national vision and missions must be interlinked with technology development and scientific achievements.

## Technology and Spirituality lead to Self-Reliance

*Science and science pursuits are borderless*

In 1893 a ship was sailing from Japan to the USA. There were hundreds of people in that ship including two significant Indian personalities—Swami Vivekananda and Jamsetji Nusserwanji Tata. Jamsetji was crossing the Atlantic Ocean to bring steel manufacturing technology for a steel plant which he wanted to set up in India. Earlier Jamsetji had gone to England for this purpose, but British steel manufacturers had refused and ridiculed him saying that if Indians would make steel, Britishers would eat it!

Swami Vivekananda asked Jamsetji the reason for his travelling to the USA. Jamsetji told him that he wanted to bring the steel industry to India. Swami Vivekananda blessed him and said that steel technology has two components—one, steel science and the other, manufacturing technology. What you can bring to this country is material technology, but you will have to build material science within the country. This triggered a dream in Jamsetji's mind.

Jamsetji was successful in bringing steel technology from the USA and the Tata Iron and Steel Company (TISCO) was established in Jamshedpur. A few years later, in 1898, Jamsetji N. Tata wrote a letter to Swami Vivekananda :

23 November 1898

Dear Swami Vivekananda,

I trust you remember me as a fellow-traveller on your voyage from Japan to Chicago. I very much recall at this moment your views on the growth of the ascetic spirit in India, and the duty, not of destroying, but of diverting it into useful channels.

I recall these ideas in connection with my scheme of Research Institute for Science of which you have doubtless heard or read. It seems to me that no better use can be made of the ascetic spirit than the establishment of monasteries or residential halls for men dominated by this spirit, where they should live with ordinary decency, and devote their lives to the cultivation of sciences—natural and humanistic. I am of the opinion that, if such a crusade in favour of an asceticism of this kind were undertaken by a competent leader, it would greatly help asceticism, science, and the good name of our country; and I know not who would make a more fitting general of such a campaign than Vivekananda. Do you think you would care to apply yourself to the mission of galvanising into life our traditions in this respect? Perhaps you had better begin with a fiery pamphlet rousing our people in this matter. I should cheerfully defray all the expenses of its publication.

Jamsetji N. Tata

*The science that we work with today must have the innovativeness, foresight and the vision for it to be the centre of technology that we develop tomorrow*

A visionary like Jamsetji with the blessings of Swamiji paved the way for the establishment of the Indian Institute of Science in 1909. The Indian Institute of Science, born out of a vision of two great minds, is a world-class institution in areas such as physics, aerospace technology, knowledge products, bio-science and bio-technology.[10]

## Religion supports Science

Most Indians, experienced and old, energetic and middle-aged, young and innocent, look to religion for solace and safety. Religions are like exquisite gardens, places full of surpassing beauty and tranquility, like sacred groves filled with beautiful birds and their melodious songs. I truly think that religions are beautiful gardens. They are enchanting islands, veritable oases for the soul and the spirit. But they are islands nevertheless.

How can we connect them so that the fragrance engulfs the whole universe? If we can connect all the islands with love and compassion in a 'garland', we will have a prosperous India and a prosperous world. I would like to recall an incident that happened four decades ago which highlights how the fusion of science and religion can lead to the transformation of religion into a spiritual force.

*Religions are enchanting islands, veritable oases for the soul and the spirit*

Prof. Vikram Sarabhai, the visionary of India's space research programme, along with Dr Homi Bhabha, was looking for a suitable site to establish a space research station in the equatorial region. These two great scientists had visited a number of places and finally selected Thumba in Kerala as the site, as it was near the equatorial region and was ideally suited for their needs.

When Prof. Vikram Sarabhai visited Thumba, he noticed that it was rather densely populated with many villages and thousands of fishermen living in and around the area. It also had a beautiful ancient church, St. Mary Magdalene Church, Pallithura and a Bishop's house. Prof. Vikram Sarabhai met several politicians and bureaucrats to get approval for Thumba as a site for the work of space science research, but he met with no success. He was then advised to see the Bishop of Trivandrum, His Excellency Rct. Rev. Dr Peter Bernard Pereira.

It was on a Saturday when Prof. Vikram Sarabhai met the Bishop. The Bishop smiled and asked him to come to the church the next day. In the Sunday morning service in the church, the Bishop told the congregation, "My children, I have a famous scientist with me who wants our church and the place where I live for the work of space science research. Dear children, science seeks truth by reasoning. In one way, science and spiritualism seek the same divine blessings for doing good for the people. My children, can we give the God's abode for a scientific mission?" There was a chorus of 'Amen' from the congregation and the whole church reverberated. And His Excellency Rct. Rev.

Dr Peter Bernard Pereira, the Bishop of Trivandrum, took the noble decision to dedicate the church in recognition of the national goal for the establishment of the Indian Space Research Organisation at Pallithura, Thumba.

It was in this very church that we housed our design centre, started the rocket assembly, the design of the filament winding machine for FRP product and the Bishop's house became our scientists' house. Later, the Thumba Equatorial Rocket Launching Station led to the establishment of the Vikram Sarabhai Space Centre and multiple space centres throughout the country.

Whenever I think of this event, I see how enlightened spiritual and scientific leaders all converge towards giving reverence to the human life. A new church and new schools were established in record time. Of course the birth of TERLS and then VSSC gave the country the capability to design, develop and produce huge world class rocket systems and subsequently, India built the capability of launching geo-synchronous, sun-synchronous and meteorology spacecraft, communication satellite, remote sensing satellite thereby providing fast communication, weather forecasting and also the ability to locate water resources for the country. Today, Prof. Vikram Sarabhai and Rev. Dr Peter Bernard Pereira are not amongst us, but they are like the flower as described in the 'Bhagwad Gita': "See the flower, how generously it distributes perfume and honey. It gives to all, gives freely of its love. When its work is done, it falls away quietly. Try to be like the flower, unassuming despite all its qualities."[11]

*If we can connect all the islands of religions with love and compassion in a 'garland', we will have a prosperous India*

On 11th May 1998, Indian scientists witnessed a great event when one after another five nuclear explosions took place. I was standing on the planet Earth on a hot sandy hill. The earth shook as though Atlas shrugged. I felt India could create energy of any magnitude but I also remembered the importance of technology in the hands of good human beings. Fortunately the central theme of our nuclear doctrine has become 'no first use'. It was born out of the civilisational heritage of our nation and inspired by the noble soul who walked the Indian soil using the weapon of *ahimsa dharma* leading to Indian independence.[12]

## Relation between Science and Spirituality

In an interactive session with students, one student wanted to know how preparation for war can be justified as a defence for peace. To this I replied that for the last 3000 years India has been invaded by many countries. Alexander invaded India followed by the Mughals, and then the French, Dutch and Portugese had set up their colonies, and finally Britain ruled India. Now that we are free

## A Spiritual Garden

An all-religion sacred herb garden called the 'Spiritual Garden' was inaugurated at Rashtrapati Bhawan on June 26, 2004. Spread over an area of approximately three-quarters of an acre the Garden houses many plants that have been commonly held in veneration by world religions.

The idea behind the Garden is to indicate the significance of the plants as a 'healing flora' for humanity.

Many of the plants are known for their healing and invigorating powers. The Garden will be an opportunity for people to forge a deeper rapport with nature and between different communities. It is thus dedicated to the reawakening in our consciousness of the intricate link with nature that lies at the core of every religion.

The Garden houses 31 plants, namely, Tetu, Arjun, Champa, Muchukunda, Dill, Olive, Grapes, Oak, Banana, Henna, Ginger, Pilu, Raktachandan, Harsingar, Chhokar, Bael, Haldi, Ashwagandha, Sahinjan, Date Palm, Pomegranate, Jasmine, Marigold, Chandan, Sorrel, Citron, Myrtle, Mint, Ashok, Amla and Shal.[16]

we need peace for our progress. When other countries have nuclear weapons India cannot sit and do '*tapas*'. Strength respects strength. Whatever we have done in defence is only to defend our freedom. At no time India either in the past or in the future would ever invade any nation. Our nuclear policy enunciates the 'no first use' principle which means defending the country is the foremost mission.[13]

*Enlightened spiritual and scientific leaders all converge towards giving reverence to human life*

To a girl who wanted to know the difference between Dr Kalam as a President and as a 'Missile Man' I answered that, while the 'Missile Man' was concerned with giving the nation strength and security, the President is concerned that a billion people should have smiles on their faces.

In an answer to yet another question from a student on the difference between science and spiritualism I explained that science tries to provide solutions for a better material life, while spiritualism looks at answers on how to lead a righteous life through such actions as prayers. Both combined lead to the creation of an enlightened citizen.[14]

Rationality and logic are intrinsic to science and spirituality. A spiritual experience is the goal of a deeply religious person whereas a major discovery or an invention is the goal of a scientific mind. If both the aspects are unified, we can then transcend to that level of thinking where there is unity of purpose and action.[15]

# TOMORROW'S CITIZENS

If India is to become
developed by 2020,
it will do so only by
riding on the shoulders
of the young[1]

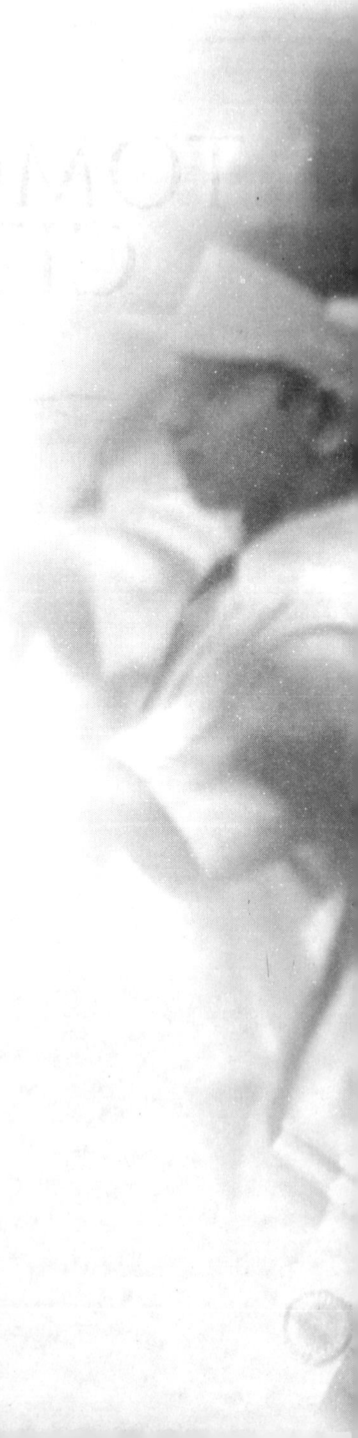

# TOMORROW'S CITIZENS

## Our Greatest Wealth

India is poised in the mission of transforming itself into a developed nation by the year 2020. The prime resource through which this transformation is possible is the 540 million youth who are below the age of twenty-five.[2]

Children and youth are the picture of a nation's future. They are our hope for tomorrow. The youth in India constitutes a sizeable, vibrant and resourceful segment of our society which has a burning desire to scale greater heights. If their energies are properly channelled, they will unleash a momentum that would propel the nation on the fast track to development. We need to carefully nurture this vast and precious human capital by making it a focal point of our planning and development process. Encompassing the needs, rights and expectations of youth to the centrestage of development should be our priority.[3]

*Encompassing the needs, rights and expectations of youth to the centrestage of development should be our priority*

Children are our greatest wealth. Every child born in the nation should be allowed to blossom. It is particularly important to provide extra care and facilities to the children including those who are not fortunate to have their families to look after them. This noble service should be promoted by all individuals and government organisations, leading to the development of enlightened citizens who will become an asset for national development.[4]

My interactions with children in India and in other nations reveal that aspirations of the young are the same, that is, to live in a peaceful, prosperous and secure nation. All of them are looking for challenging missions, good role models and leaders who can be their guiding spirit. A combination of knowledge, enthusiasm and hard work of the youth is a great dynamic fire for transforming the nation.[5]

## Education is the Right of Every Child

Education is the most important element for growth and prosperity of a nation. Yet

## Declaration by the Citizens

We have to recognise and value the importance of children, for which all citizens should take an oath.

- Children are our precious wealth.
- We will give equal importance to male and female children in providing education and rights for growth.
- For health and prosperity we will have a small family.
- Earnings come from hard work. We will not waste them on gambling and liquor.
- We need to tell our children about the importance of education, as learning gives knowledge and knowledge makes the children succeed.
- We need to jointly protect our forests and prevent pollution.
- We will plant at least five trees/ saplings.
- We will become role models for our children.[6]

we have 350 million people who need to be made literate. Children who belong to weaker sections of our society are undernourished, and only a small percentage of them manages to complete eight years of satisfactory education. We need to think specifically for them. Education is indeed a fundamental right of every Indian child. Can we allow the situation to continue in which millions of children are forced into lifelong poverty?

An important area of concern is the unequal access to educational resources, which still exists after almost six decades of independence. For example, I have seen in our villages three types of families. The fortunuate ones, who, due to their economic well-being, realise the importance of educating the young ones at any cost, guide them at all critical stages. Then there are those families who might realise the importance of education, but are not aware of the opportunities in time, nor of the procedures and ways to realise these opportunities for their children. There is a third category of families who are economically weak and do not realise the value of education and hence for generations together their children are neglected and continue to live in poverty. It is essential that we enlighten them and create widespread awareness of education among all sections of society particularly in rural areas and among the urban poor.

*Though the present academic system may give students a lot of workload, but it should not prevent them from dreaming*

It is reported that 39 per cent of children drop out from school after studying upto the 5th class and 55 per cent drop out after studying up to the 8th class. This situation needs remedial action, especially since assent has been accorded for the 86th Constitution Amendment Act, Right to Education Bill for children between the age group of five and fourteen years. But an Act alone cannot achieve the goal unless the education is delivered in a manner relevant to the people to whom it is addressed.[7]

*The 'dream-thought-action' philosophy is what I would like to be inculcated in each and every student*

## Dream–Thought–Action

The challenge in the mission of Developed India calls for an important, cohesive and focused effort of the young. A nation is great because of the way its people think. Particularly the young population of India must have a big aim; small aim is a crime.

Though the present academic system may give students a lot of workload, it should not prevent them from dreaming. It doesn't prevent them from working hard to acquire knowledge. Hard work and perseverance are beautiful angels who will support you.

In the 1960s Prof. Vikram Sarabhai, the visionary of our space programme, put forth the vision that India should design and develop its own communication satellites, remote-sensing satellites and launch them in polar orbits from the Indian soil for mapping Indian natural resources. Today his dream has become true. The nation is capable of developing any type of space system.

*Dream, dream, dream,*
*Your dreams will transform into thoughts,*
*The thoughts will result in actions.*
*And you will succeed.*[8]

Encourage all children to dream for themselves. Unless they have dreams they will not be motivated to attain them. Slowly, you will find that, with proper effort, dreams will transform into thoughts and with effort and labour, these thoughts can be transformed into action. Success is possible only when we have a commitment to action. This 'dream-thought-action' philosophy is what I would like to be inculcated in each and every one of the students.[9]

*The young population of India must have a big aim, small aim is a crime*

It is not a disgrace to not reach the stars, but it is a disgrace to have no stars to reach for.[10]

## Knowledge–Sweat–Perseverance

One cannot stop at thinking and asking questions. There is need to act to solve the problems and that requires hard work and perseverance.

As President and earlier as a scientist, life has taught me the importance of three qualities knowledge, sweat and perseverance.[11]

Our country has a very bright future and all of us, especially the children, who will be the leaders of tomorrow have to work hard. The vision of a Developed India will not come on its own. It will not be gifted to us by someone but we have to work and work hard to achieve the goals which we have set for ourselves. It is only through sweat and toil that we will be able to make India stand proudly among the comity of developed nations. If India is to become developed by 2020, it will do so only by riding on the shoulders of the young.[12]

## Role of Students

A 'Developed India' is no more a vision. The largest beneficiary of this dream when realised will be the young. Hence it is important that you contribute in its initial stages of realisation and shape it to the best of your abilities within your academic and family confines. The biggest concern of the parents and the children in your age group is the job prospect after you complete your education. Without worrying about minor variations in the subjects of your pursuit, your opportunities and future will be brighter if you excel in whatever subject you undertake to study. At the frontier there are no borders. The employment opportunities are many, but when a person becomes very selective and wants only a government job, then there are tremendous constraints. If you open up your thoughts to entrepreneurship, design, industry, direct participation in agriculture with innovative ideas, making IT products, etc. the opportunities are unlimited. The most important thing for the young generation is to make up its mind to contribute in all sectors through the tools of knowledge and physical contribution.

One of the important indicators of a developed nation is the literacy level. Educating a nation of a billion people is not a small task. It requires the participation of all the stakeholders starting from the young. Many of you are fortunate enough to attend good schools for a quality education. But many of your brothers and sisters are not that fortunate, particularly those from the villages.

*It is not a disgrace to not reach the stars, but it is a disgrace to have no stars to reach for*

A good sign of a developed nation is that 'people who have' work hard to bridge the divide between themselves and 'those who have not'. One way of doing this is for your school to adopt a village near you. Each one of you could visit the village on holidays and contribute to the removal of illiteracy of at least two persons and light the quest for knowledge in them.[13]

Further, children can plant at least ten trees either in the school campus or in their houses.

A few years from now, every one of us would be able to work in a serene environment that would facilitate creative thoughts and actions.

Students can take care of the elderly members, ailing persons and be the friends of differently challenged people. Such noble gestures create a conducive and harmonious atmosphere for development activities. Whatever work you do, put your 100 per cent sincere efforts to complete the same. Discipline, determination and dedication lead to success.

A *kural* by Thiruvalluvar expresses it beautifully :

ஆக்கம் அதர்வினாய்ச் செல்லும் அசைவிலா
ஊக்க முடையா னுழை.

This means that success and wealth will seek out their way and reach the person who has an inflexible will and systematic diligence. Good fortune will search out the man who has an indomitable spirit as well as an unremitting zeal.[14]

## When can I sing a Song of India

When I travel across our nation, when I hear the sound of the waves of the three seas around the shores of my country, when I experience the breeze of the winds from the mighty

## Oath for Students

- I will pursue my education with dedication and I will excel in it.
- I will plant at least five saplings and shall ensure their growth through constant care.
- I will constantly endeavour to remove the pain of my suffering brethren.
- I will work for becoming an enlightened citizen and make my family righteous.
- I will always be a friend of the mentally and physically challenged and will work hard to make them feel normal, like the rest of us.
- I promise that I will work hard with honesty to transform my country into a developed country.[15]

Himalayas, when I see the biodiversity of the North East and our islands and when I feel the warmth of the western desert, I hear the voice of the youth asking, "When can I sing the song of India?" What can be the answer?

*At the frontier there are no borders*

If the youth have to sing the song of India, India should become a developed country which is free from poverty, illiteracy and unemployment and is buoyant with economic prosperity, national security and internal harmony.[16]

During the last four years I have interacted with thousands of schoolchildren. Some of my friends had launched a website in my name, through which I exchange views, particularly with the young within the country and abroad. I had put forth two points on the website for the young to share their thoughts. The first point was : India has been a developing country for more than half a century, what will you do to make it a 'Developed India'?

The second point was : When can I sing a song of India? There were some important suggestions that I received in response. One student from Meghalaya had responded, "I will become a teacher (rather a Professor of Engineering) since I am good at it, as well as enjoy teaching, and I believe that one of the best ways in which to serve any nation is to be either a professor or a soldier among many other professions." What a noble thought! Such beautiful thoughts can come only from a beautiful place like Meghalaya.

*The young people are looking for challenging missions, good role models and leaders who can be their guiding spirit*

Another young girl from Kerala said, "A single flower makes no garland. I will make my countrymen develop love for the nation and work for making a garland of developed India." A twenty-year-old boy from Goa responded, "I would become an electron and like an electron in the orbit I will work ceaselessly for my country from now onwards."

With reference to the second point I had put forth, a young man from Atlanta says, "When India builds the capability to put sanction against any country if needed, then I will sing a song of India." What the young man meant was that economic strength brings prosperity, accompanied by national strength.

The cross-section of people of this young age group has an inspired mind to make the nation great. It is important to recognise that India has a population of 540 million young people. This is a big force. Creating a powerful vision for the nation will bring the force and energy of the young into action.[17]

## The Song of Youth

*As a young citizen of India,*
*Armed with technology, knowledge*
*and love for my nation,*
*I realize, small aim is a crime.*
*I will work and sweat for a great vision,*
*The vision of transforming India*
*into a developed nation,*
*Powered by economic strength with value system.*
*I am one of the citizens of a billion,*
*Only the vision will ignite the billion souls.*
*It has entered into me,*
*the ignited soul compared to any resource*
*is the most powerful resource*
*On the earth, above the earth and under the earth.*
*I will keep the lamp of knowledge burning*
*To achieve the vision—Developed India.*

If we work and sweat for the great vision with ignited minds, the transformation leading to the birth of a vibrant Developed India will take place. This song, when sung in our own beautiful languages, will unite our minds and hearts.[18]

# EMPOWERED WOMEN

When women are empowered, a society with stability is assured. Gone are the days when women were considered subservient or secondary in almost all walks of life compared to men. It has now amply been proved that women are capable of executing any job as efficiently as men, if not more so[1]

राष्ट्रीय सेवा योजना
NATIONAL SERVICE SCHEME

# EMPOWERED WOMEN

## Women and Nation Building

In our country women constitute 48 per cent of the total population. If this 48 per cent contributes to the national development, then the national vision of transforming India into a developed nation by 2020 will be that much nearer.

Nowadays women are shining in every field. They are becoming doctors, engineers, advocates, teachers, political leaders, administrators, police officials, professionals and have also joined the armed forces. Enlightened women are particularly important for nation building since their thoughts, their way of working and value system will lead to faster development of a good family, good society and a good nation.[2]

When women are empowered, a society with stability will get assured. For this women education has to be given the highest priority. There is need to ensure the continuity of secondary education and university education for girls, and distance education packages have to be evolved to cater to women in remote areas.[3]

After completing basic general education, a girl should be able to opt for a vocational training programme which will enable her to seek either self-employment or employment in establishments. This has to be done keeping in mind the aptitude of the girl and the need for such skills as required for a particular occupation. The emphasis should be on making every woman educated and economically self-dependent as early as possible.[4]

*India has a long tradition of giving equal opportunity to women to excel in every field*

## Women with Pioneering Missions

India has a long tradition of giving equal opportunity to women to excel in every field. Indian women had voting rights far earlier than most developed countries. Even in earlier times we had celebrated warriors and rulers of kingdoms in India such as Rani of Jhansi and Rani Mangamma. Amongst the scientists and natural philosophers who contributed immensely to science in ancient India, Gargi, who was born three thousand years ago, Leelavati of the 12th century and Maitrayee stand out. During the foreign occupation of India the role of Indian women had been somewhat subdued, but independent India has started to see the resurgence of its women.[s]

*Women are shining in every field*

During the course of my travels I have met many women who have done pioneering work in their areas of specialisation. Amongst them are Kanchan Choudhry Bhattacharya, the first woman to become the Director General of Police of Uttaranchal. Two very senior air force and naval officers, Air Marshal P Bandopadhyay, Director General, Medical Services (Air) and Surg. Vice Admiral Punita Arora, Director General, Medical Services (Navy) are doing pioneering work in the medical field. Capt. Sipra Majumdar and Capt. Ashwini A S Pawar are the first women summiteers to climb Mt. Everest from the northern side. I also talked to the women army officers in the freezing temperatures of Kargil and appreciate their courage and perseverance for succeeding in their missions. Dr Shanta who has been recently selected for the Ramon Magsaysay award was responsible for setting up the radiation oncology department in the Cancer Institute and organised the first-ever hospital tumour registry in India. She also established the first paediatric oncology unit. Above all the Nobel laureate Mother Teresa represents the embodiment of service to humanity. These women should become role models for all Indian women.[6]

Rohini Devi is a very senior scientist working in the Defence Research and Development Organisation. One of the interesting products which she has developed is the carbon brake disc for Light Combat Aircraft (LCA). The project team was wavering whether to follow the option of importing the brake pad or to continue with the indigenous development within a strict time frame. All over the world it has been reported that such a brake pad has not been developed apart from a few developed countries. One leading manufacturer from the West challenged the programme saying it would be nearly impossible to make it in the country and offered a total solution at a very heavy price.

But the project team took courage and encouraged the indigenous effort being piloted by Rohini Devi. As expected in many such missions, initially the product did not give the required wear-rate though it was meeting the required brake performance. That is where the team headed by Rohini Devi toiled and through persevering scientific endeavour overcame the barriers and realised the wear-rate prescribed by the project. This technology solely developed in the country has numerous spin-offs and applications in the civilian sector. Now the same team is working on carbon nano-tubes and is also developing functionally graded material which will eventually revolutionise the materials used in aerospace and defence. This shows the courage, the innovative spirit and commitment of a woman scientist to 'make the impossible, possible'.

The Akash missile system is guided by the phased array radar—Rajendra. This radar can simultaneously track multiple aircrafts and also guide multiple missiles towards these targets. The crucial technology to achieve this capability is the 'phase shifter'. Rajendra Radar has 4500 phase shifters. These phase shifters were not commercially available because of restriction by the developed countries. This phase shifter was designed and developed by Prof Bharati Bhat, a well-known and respected scientist of the Indian Institute of Technology, Delhi, with her team. Today, India has the phased array radar technology which is at par with that available in the developed countries.

*Every organisation has to be made aware that there is no difference between men and women*

One of the toughest endurance tests for any human is to undertake space travel. It is commendable that a girl, who was born in a sleepy town in Haryana, took up the study of aeronautical engineering and dreamt of being called the child of the galaxy. She worked hard and became the first Indian woman to become a member of the space shuttle. While on the space shuttle she flew for an incredible 760 hours and conducted advanced scientific experiments in space. Kalpana Chawla is an example of how single-minded dedication can lead to the realisation of childhood dreams, however complex and tough they may be.[7]

When Dr Vikram Sarabhai, the founder of ISRO (Indian Space Research Organisation) passed away there was a near crisis situation in terms of creating a management system for the space programme. Prof. Kamala Choudhary, a renowned management expert from the Indian Institute of Management, Ahmedabad was given the task by Prof. M G K Menon the then Chairman of ISRO, to reorganise with the changed environment and the mission. She started her work by interviewing different cross-sections of scientists, technicians and staff and drew up a reorganisation management plan for ISRO which was unique and stands even today. It had two important aspects:

empowering the scientist and creating people-centric missions, taking into account the organisation's vision and people's dreams and aspirations. The result of such an empowered organisation plan electrified ISRO to achieve major milestones and it has become a very successful organisation.[8]

## Equal Partners

During a visit to Himachal Pradesh, Vijaya Sharma of the Rajkiya Kanya Mahavidyalya asked me what a girl's role should be in independent India. I replied there is really no difference in the roles of men and women as they are equal partners in national development.[9]

This is the era of women empowerment. Gone are the days when women were considered subservient or secondary in almost all walks of life compared to men. It has now amply been proved that women are capable of executing any job as efficiently as men, if not more so.

## Gender-Sensitivity Training

However, there is a need to have training programmes on gender-sensitive issues for men and women with an objective to highlight the strengths of men and women individually and how both of them can effectively collaborate and contribute to the common goals of an organisation. Such training should address the special needs of women and how the system has to pay attention to maintain harmony in the society. This will remove many of the misconceptions and misperceptions among employees. By paying attention to planning of the tasks for men and women, their working hours, sharing of responsibility and performance, it will help bring about a healthy understanding of the contribution of men by women and vice versa in an organisational set-up.

Every organisation has to be made aware that there is no difference between men and women. The work allocation can be done on the basis of a roster, randomly for men and women, as is being done by the High Court and the Supreme Court. Such random allocation of tasks will remove the feeling that women are not being treated as equals. Also, there should be a meeting with all the personnel once in a month to hear specific grievances of individual officers. Based on these grievances there must be immediate corrective action if a grievance is found to be genuine. Such a transparent system will definitely promote confidence among all personnel, particularly the women, if there are any gender issues. Periodically senior officers should highlight the importance of teamwork between men and women during their inspection visits to various units. While planning an operation it is always desirable to have a mixed team of men and women.

*Women are equal partners in national development*

Women must be given the leadership in some cases and men should take the leadership in some others.[10]

### Emerging Women

When we think of future women professionals and leaders with an urge to participate in the national movement, I am reminded of Mahakavi Subramaniya Bharatiar, who in 1910 composed this poem envisioning women of India :

*She walks with raised head,*
*With her eyes looking straight,*
*She has her principles,*
*Unafraid of anybody!*
*She has a lofty and knowledge based pride,*
*Such cultured women,*
*Don't falter from the chosen path,*
*She drives ignorance away.*
*She welcomes the bliss of life,*
*With learned mind,*
*This is the Dharma*
*Of emerging woman.*

The dream of the poet, I am sure, will become a reality of life for all the women of our nation.[11]

# TOWARDS A KNOWLEDGE SOCIETY

Knowledge has always been the prime mover of prosperity and power. The acquisition of knowledge has therefore been the thrust area throughout the world and sharing the experience of knowledge is a unique culture of our country[1]

# TOWARDS A KNOWLEDGE SOCIETY

## Birth of a Knowledge Society

During the last century, the world has undergone a change from being an agricultural society where manual labour was the critical factor to an industrial society where the management of technology, capital and labour provide the competitive advantage. And in the last decade the information era was born, where connectivity and software products are the prime drivers of the economy of a nation.

In the 21st century, a new society is emerging where knowledge is the primary production resource instead of capital and labour.

Efficient utilisation of knowledge can create comprehensive wealth for a nation and also improve the quality of life in the form of better health, education, infrastructure and other social indicators.

*Ancient knowledge is a unique resource of our country and it is essential to leverage it both for our national well being and to mark our global presence*

The ability to create and maintain a knowledge infrastructure, develop knowledge workers and enhance their productivity through creation, growth and exploitation of new knowledge will be the key factors in deciding the prosperity of this Knowledge Society. Whether a nation has arrived at the stage of knowledge society or not is judged by the way a country effectively deals with knowledge creation and knowledge deployment in all sectors of the economy.[2]

## Dimensions of a Knowledge Society

In the knowledge economy the objective of a society changes from fulfilling the basic needs of all-round development to empowerment.

> The education system instead of going by textbook teaching will be promoted by creative and interactive self learning, with focus on values, merit and quality.
>
> The workers, instead of being skilled or semi-skilled, will be knowledgeable, self-empowered and flexibly skilled.

Work, instead of being structured and hardware driven, will be less structured and more software driven.

Management style will emphasise delegation rather than giving command.

The impact on environment and ecology will be strikingly less compared to industrial economy.

Finally, the economy will be knowledge driven and not industry driven.[3]

## Components of a Knowledge Society

*In the 21st century a new society is emerging where knowledge is the primary production resource instead of capital and labour*

Knowledge society has two very important components – societal transformation and wealth generation.

A national task team has identified core areas that will spearhead our march towards a knowledge society. These are: information technology, bio-technology, space technology, weather forecasting, disaster management, tele-medicine and tele-education, technologies to produce native knowledge products, service sector and infotainment. We need to rapidly develop competency in these areas so that the resulting progress and development can help bring about a societal transformation.

Wealth generation, which is the second component for establishing a knowledge society, has to be woven around the identified national core areas. The methodology of wealth generation in these core areas has to be able to meet an export target set at 50 billion dollars by the year 2008, especially using the Information Technology (IT) sector and simultaneously developing capability to generate IT products worth 30 billion dollars domestically to pump in for societal transformation.

Evolution of policy and administrative procedures, changes in regulatory methods, identification of patents and most importantly creation of young and dynamic leaders are the components that need to be in place for this. In order to generate wealth, it is essential that simultaneously a citizen-centric approach to evolution of business policy, user-driven technology generation and intensified industry-lab-academy linkages have also to be established.[4]

While a knowledge society has a two-dimensional objective of societal transformation and wealth generation, a third dimension emerges when India has to transform into a knowledge power. The hard-earned wealth and the transformed society, which are the two pillars on which the knowledge society is supported, have to be protected in order to sustain a knowledge society. Thus knowledge protection is the third dimension.

## Preserving Traditional Knowledge

There is a great wealth of knowledge in villages which is to be found in their history, folk songs, cultural traditions and arts, traditional medicinal practices and marketing information and methods. Such information presently is being transmitted through word of mouth but with each passing generation it is being gradually lost. It is essential to preserve and carry forward this knowledge base for the benefit of future generations.

India has rich information relating to literature, music, traditional systems of medicine and science embedded in palm leaves and it is necessary to preserve this valuable information. Merely scanning the palm leaves would not be very useful because the number of people who can read these palm leaves and interpret the meanings, and identify the plants and stones mentioned in them is dwindling. Even those few who can read, cannot write very well, and also may not be fluent in entering this information into the computer in digital forms. The optical character recognition of these ancient scripts is also a very tough problem, almost intractable technically. I suggest that, for every palm leaf scanned, we record in audio the information read by experts which can then be put on the web and invite experts to provide free and fair commentary and validate every palm leaf data. This data can also be used for creating a new generation of palm leaf reading experts—a species that has almost vanished.[5]

## Digital Library Initiatives

*Information that is static is of no value*

Digital libraries are not the digital equivalents of the present-day library. These would include, besides books, manuscripts and journals, which are sources of explicit knowledge, information and our heritage in all other forms including speeches, folk songs, paintings and carvings, all of which comprise implicit knowledge. It is important that we take on this mission of integrating all forms of knowledge and culture into our digital library.[6]

There is a mission to create a portal for a Digital Library of India piloted by the Ministry of Information Technology with the IISc and Carnegie Mellon University as partners for fostering creativity and free access to all human knowledge. This library was launched in 2003 and so far twenty centres are operational throughout the country, and over 50,000 books have been digitised of which nearly 30,000 are in nine different Indian languages.

The advantage of a digital library is that it provides equitable access to knowledge to all the people, irrespective of place, caste, creed, colour or economic status. A digital library unites rather than divides. It is where the past meets the present and creates a future. A digital library indeed would combat the Digital Divide which is of great concern for us in India.[7]

## Empowerment through Connectivity

*Blended knowledge is better knowledge*

Connectivity is strength. Connectivity is wealth. Connectivity is progress.

The core of empowerment for the prosperity of one billion people is the connectivity and partnership between governmental and multiple institutions in the public and private domains. The strength of this partnership for collaborative growth and economic prosperity is facilitated by the free flow of knowledge and information in a seamless manner cutting across levels and boundaries and embracing all walks of life in the three sectors of the economy, viz., agriculture, manufacturing and services.

In a proposed model for development, the inter-connectivity among these three sectors of the economy is brought about by four grids, namely, knowledge grid, health grid, e-governance grid and the rural grid. This system of grids will bring prosperity to 700 million people in the rural areas and 300 million plus people in the urban areas. In the process, it will ensure that the lives of 260 million people below the poverty line are transformed.

### Knowledge Grid

India is now in the process of creating virtual universities and institutions for knowledge sharing, knowledge dissemination and knowledge re-use. While it is known

that the virtual universities provide us with technologies of the future and the most economic way of achieving high quality education in the country, they are no substitute to the campus-based education. The challenge before the virtual universities is to provide the best of both the worlds.

The three tools of learning are lectures, libraries and laboratories. Unlike in the real world, where the equitable access is always the democratic average, in the virtual universities the equitable access always means the equitable access to the best resources available across the network, be it teachers, library, laboratory. In effect, the network brings the best of its resources to every one of its participants.

But this requires increasing bandwidth from a few 100s of kilobytes for the lectures to a few megabytes for the formal digital libraries and the informal world of knowledge from the Internet, to gigabytes of connectivity for remote laboratories in the world of high precision science and engineering. As the bandwidth becomes cheaper and available in abundance, universities should be able to run remote instruments and complex facilities. These are applications that can make a difference in how we engage in teaching, learning and research in higher education and will ultimately provide equitable access to the entire education system.

The bandwidth is the demolisher of imbalances and a great leveller in the knowledge society. We have rich knowledge institutions but what we have to add is connectivity throughout the country to provide uniform access of knowledge in different regions leading to the creation of a National Knowledge Grid.

*Bandwidth is the demolisher of imbalances and a great leveller in the knowledge society*

## Health Grid

There is a need to establish a National Health Grid, connecting various healthcare institutions in both the super speciality and general medicine areas. Healthcare training institutes and medical research institutions networked to the health grid will enable unique case studies and experiences to be exchanged between the super specialists through this health grid. It will also be possible to conduct conferences of specialist doctors from multi-centres to discuss the critical disease patterns and provide treatment.

## E-Governance Grid

Good governance is being recognised as an important goal by most countries across the world and many specific initiatives for open government have been taken. The Internet revolution has proved to be a powerful tool for good governance initiatives as it makes it possible to provide services anytime anywhere. Delivery of services to citizens is considered a primary function of the government. Particularly in a democratic nation of a billion people like India, e-governance should enable seamless access to information and seamless flow of information across the State and Central governments.

**Typical scenario:** I visualise an election scenario, where a candidate files his nomination from a particular constituency. Immediately the election officer verifies his authenticity from the national citizen identity database. His education credentials come from the university records. His track record of employment comes from various employers

with whom he has worked. Information about his income and wealth resources comes from the income-tax department. Details of his property record come from the registration of land authority across the country. His civic consciousness and citizenship behaviour comes from the police crime record and the judicial system.

*A digital library provides equitable access to knowledge to all the people, irrespective of place, caste, creed, colour or economic status.*

All these details arrive at the computer terminal of the election officer within a few seconds with the help of software tools crawling across the various State and Central government web service directories collecting the necessary information and presenting it in real-time without any bias. Artificial intelligence software analyses the candidate's credentials and gives a rating on how successful he will be as a politician. The election officer sitting in a remote block of the country decides on the eligibility of the candidate and the election process starts. All the voters vote from their home through virtual polling booths.

Is it a dream? Is it possible? If possible, when shall we have it? Can we provide good governance to our one billion people? Can the governance speed up the delivery system? Can the governance differentiate between genuine transactions and spurious transactions? Can the governance ensure immediate action in genuine cases which satisfy the checklist for a particular service and take penal action against spurious transactions? Can this be done by e-governance at a cost affordable by our nation? If we have this system implemented then I would call this a true e-governance system for the citizen.

*A digital library unites rather than divides*

To establish such a system, we need a high bandwidth broadband connectivity across the many government departments such as the state and the district administration, election commission, universities, banks, home/police departments, insurance companies, etc. This scenario requires vertical and horizontal grids established across various institutions so that we can draw and feed information from these grids for seamless flow of data to achieve the goal of good governance.

## Rural Grid

I visualise establishment of a village knowledge centre in the village panchayat to empower the villagers with knowledge and to act as a local centre for knowledge connectivity for the villagers within the overall framework of Providing Urban Amenities to Rural Areas (PURA).
The village knowledge centre should provide essential data required for the targeted population such as farmers, fishermen, craftsmen, traders, businessmen, entrepreneurs, unemployed youth and students. Local relevance of information offered is the most critical factor. Users have

simple information needs but often these pose a tough problem for system integrators because of the need for constant updation of data.

Trained manpower with experience has to be deployed to generate information which can explain to the people in simple terms the meteorological, weather and marketing data on fish, agricultural and other rural commodities. These data have to come from various connected institutions which provide service to the people on a real time basis. But the transformation of data into user-friendly information on a regular updated basis is the real challenge.

*Digital library is where the past meets the present and creates a future*

Another focus of the village knowledge centre should be to empower the youth to undertake development tasks of the villages and establish rural enterprises which will provide large-scale employment. So, it is essential that these centres should be able to provide skills and knowledge through linkages with industry, banking and marketing institutions because blended knowledge is better knowledge.

## Realising the Mission of a Developed Nation

The total land area of India is around 3.3 million square kilometres with 7000 kilometres of coastline. The altitude of the country varies from the sea level to 8,600 metres. The entire area is spread across deserts, hills, mountains, seashores, islands, valleys and plains. Out of the billion plus population in the country, 70 per cent live in six lakh villages. India is a nation endowed with natural and competitive advantages as also certain distinctive competencies. But these are scattered in isolated pockets and awareness of which is inadequate.

We need a societal transformation and sustainable development for our growth. These two aspects are realisable in a time-bound manner only through creation of a knowledge society, which alone will empower the entire nation.

India has the potential to become a knowledge society. Electronic and knowledge connectivity is the key to realise this goal. Connecting a billion people throws up multiple challenges. We have to be ready to meet these challenges and make India a developed nation.[8]

# BUILDING A DEVELOPED INDIA

We should all create a nation that is one of the best places to live in on this earth and which brings smiles to a billion faces[1]

# BUILDING A DEVELOPED INDIA

### The Nation is Bigger than any Individual

The independence movement created and nurtured the concept that the nation is bigger than any individual or any system of organisation. But during the last few decades this national spirit has been at a low ebb. What we need today is that all political parties cooperate with one another and answer the overwhelming question facing all of us : "When will India become a developed nation?"[2]

There is need to have coherent thinking among all the members of the society. All of us need to think and realise that the nation is greater than any one individual or organisation. There is a mindset among many of us that 'we cannot do it'. However, my experiences with many different institutions in the country and the observations of the results of some of them working in the mission-mode projects have shown that, whenever we have decided to achieve certain goals with clear targets, we have always achieved them. I have seen this both in the private and public sectors—if they decide to take up a task as a mission, they always succeed.[3]

## Inculcate a Sense of National Pride

When you are haunted with cultural invasions through the media and elsewhere, think of yourself as children of civilisation bliss. We have withstood multiple invasions and though many dynasties ruled us, today India is free from invasions and is independent. We have absorbed the best of cultures from successive invasions and evolved great qualities of leadership to manage the nation of a billion people with diversity in every aspect of life.[4] Now we should not allow any religion or any individual fanaticism to endanger our nation.

*Our sweat will transform developing India into a Developed India*

There has to be unflinching commitment to the principle of secularism, which is the cornerstone of our nationhood and which is the key feature of our civilisational strength. Leaders of all religions should echo one message, that of unity of the minds and hearts of our people, and soon we will see the golden age of our country.[5]

We are self-reliant in food production, we make our own communication satellites and launch our own remote-sensing satellites. When India became a nuclear weapon state and a missile power, developed nations imposed economic and technological sanctions against us. But we withstood and combated with our agricultural, technological and industrial might and, above all, with the courage of our people. Keep this spirit and multiply it with dynamic momentum.

When you look around the world, you may sometimes get discouraged to think that you belong to one of the hundreds of developing nations and not to the so called developed 'G-8'. At that time think of the billion ignited Indian minds. This is the most powerful resource compared to any resource on the earth, above the earth and below the earth. Our sweat will transform developing India into a developed nation. That is the vision of the Millennium Mission 2020—a Developed India.[6]

## The First Vision

The first vision of independence in 1857 triggered a process of change driven by a strong sense of patriotism and sacrifice with a unity of mind and purpose.

There was a desire in many Indians to excel and surpass foreigners in every field of life. This remarkable phenomenon, which manifested itself as the need for self-expression became a dominant motivating force among the Indian youth during the national movement. It was a part of the national movement to assert oneself and show the West that we were equal to them. The first vision of the freedom movement generated top-class leaders in every walk of life, be it politics, public life, music, poetry, literature or science.

*Any country is as good as its citizens; their ethos, their values and their character will be reflected in the country's make-up*

## The Second Vision

Now, after almost six decades of independence, aspirations are mounting that India should become a developed country. This is the second vision for the nation. How can we prepare ourselves for this challenge?[7]

## Transforming Vision into Missions

Our nation is going through a major challenge of uplifting 260 million of its people who are below the poverty line. They need habitat, food, healthcare and employment. While the national Gross Domestic Product (GDP) is growing at the rate of about 6 per cent per annum, economists suggest that to uplift people below the poverty line our economy has to grow at the rate of 10 per cent per annum consistently over the next decade.

**Integrated action :** Five areas have been identified where India has core competency for integrated action: agriculture and food processing; reliable and quality electric power, surface transport and infrastructure; education and healthcare; information and communication technology; and strategic sectors. These five areas are closely interrelated and rapid development in these would lead to national, food and economic security.[8]

*A vast pool of human resources with a large proportion of a young population is a unique strength of our nation*

**Engines for growth :** Emphasis should be on full utilisation of natural and human resources of the nation to meet the demands of the growing society. We should also remember that about 50 per cent of our population is comprised of young people with aspirations for better living standards. Value addition to agriculture, manufacturing and service sectors, building the national core competence and technologies will lead to additional high income employment potential. The engines for growth will be accelerated by launching of the five national missions, viz., water, energy, education and skills, infrastructure and employment generation that will enable achievement of 10 per cent GDP growth rate per annum.[9]

## Profile of Developed India

My visualisation of a competitive Developed India has the following attributes :

- A nation where the rural and urban divide has been reduced to a thin line.
- A nation where there is an equitable distribution of energy and quality water.
- A nation where agriculture, industry and service sector work together in symphony, absorbing technology, thereby resulting in sustained wealth generation leading to higher employment potential.
- A nation where education is not denied to any meritorious candidate because of societal or economic discrimination.
- A nation which is the best destination for the most talented scholars and scientists from all over the world.
- A nation where the best healthcare is available to the billion population and communicable diseases like AIDS/TB, water and vector-borne diseases, cardiac diseases and cancer are extinct.
- A nation where the governance uses the best of the technologies to be responsive, transparent, easily accessible and simple in rules, and thereby corruption free.
- A nation where poverty has been totally alleviated, illiteracy and crime against women are eradicated and the society is unalienated.

*The precious asset of a company or a country is the skill, ingenuity and imagination of its people*

- A nation that is prosperous, healthy, secure, peaceful and happy.
- A nation that is one of the best places to live in on the earth and which brings smiles to a billion plus faces.[10]

## Development with Democracy

This vision of a Developed India needs to be achieved with parliamentary democracy which is the core of our governance system. The basic structure of our Constitution has stood the test of time. The first and foremost task is to respect and uphold the constitutional processes in the best interest of our people and our nation.

*Repeating what we did before for several decades with more of the same may not be the way to proceed further*

India is a union of states based on the framework of co-operative federalism. Within the co-operative framework there is also a requirement to develop competitive strengths for the states so that they can excel at the national and global level. Competitiveness helps in ensuring economic and managerial efficiency and spurs creativity to meet new challenges which are essential to survive and prosper in the fast-changing world of today. Freedom to move, freedom to think and freedom to express are ingrained in the freedom to live; it is also enshrined in our Constitution. There cannot be inter-state barriers or inter-regional curbs as these would snap the thread of unity. All of us will have to work together to create a conducive atmosphere for unhindered progress of developmental activities.

Along with speedy development aimed at elimination of poverty and unemployment, national security has to be recognised by every Indian as a national priority. Indeed, making India strong and self-reliant economically, socially and militarily is our foremost duty to our motherland, to ourselves and to our future generations.[11]

Creating a standardised quality education with value system across the population leading to a corruption-free society is a challenging problem needing out-of-the-box unusual solutions. A fair and equitable access to a judicial system that is sensitive to changes in technology and society; pollution-free and energy-efficient urban transport systems that are scaleable nationwide are also equally challenging problems that need immediate attention. Policy decisions and appropriate actions to overcome such challenges will be the typical bricks that would be required to build the edifice of a developed nation by 2020.[12]

## Leveraging Natural Resources

The nation's strengths predominantly reside in its natural and human resources. In natural resources, India is endowed with a vast coastline rich with marine resources and oil wealth. As far as minerals are concerned, apart from conventional material resources, it is well known that India has the largest deposits of precious metal ores and coal. India ranks among the top few nations with a rich bio-diversity.

Knowledge based value addition for these natural resources would mean enriching the country and producing and exporting value-added products rather than merely the raw materials. Use of information technology for commercialisation in the form of tele-medicine, tele-education, e-governance and marketing can increase our outreach and speed enormously.

Ancient knowledge is a unique resource of our country and it is essential to leverage this both for national well-being and to mark our global presence.

## Developing People

A vast pool of human resources, with a large proportion of a young population, is a unique strength of our nation. Through education and training, unskilled manpower can be transformed into skilled and creative wealth generators particularly in the service sectors and agro industries. Knowledge-intensive industries can be generated out of our existing industries by injecting demand for high-level software and hardware personnel which would bring tremendous value addition. It is said, 'the precious asset of a company or a country is the skill, ingenuity and imagination of its people.' With globalisation, this will become more important because everybody will have access to world class technology and the key distinguishing feature will be the ability of people in different countries to use their imagination to make the best use of the technology. Indeed development and innovative use of multiple technologies with mission-oriented projects and transparent management structure will catapult India into a developed nation.[13]

## Transforming Rural India

Nearly 700 million people of India live in the rural areas in six lakh villages. Connectivity of village complexes providing economic opportunities to all segments of people is an urgent requirement to bridge the rural-urban divide, generate employment and enhance rural prosperity. Repeating what we did before for several decades with more of the same may not be the way to proceed further. We need to innovate to increase connectivities to the villages, making clusters out of them even while retaining their individualities.

*All of us need to think and realise that the nation is greater than any one individual or organisation*

The integrated methods which will bring prosperity to rural India are : the physical connectivity of the village clusters through quality roads and transport; electronic

*We have to collectively inculcate a positive attitude of what we can do for our country so that together we will be able to benefit ourselves*

connectivity through tele-communication with high bandwidth fibre optic cables reaching the rural areas from urban cities and through Internet kiosks; knowledge connectivity through education, skill training for farmers, artisans and craftsmen and entrepreneurship programmes. These three connectivities will lead to economic connectivity through starting of enterprises with the help of banks, micro credits and marketing of the products. The integrated method envisages a mission mode empowered management structure with executive powers at the local implementation levels and by reducing the transactional costs through simplification of procedures of governance.[14]

## Values and Attitude

The need of the hour is disciplined action by all citizens. This will lead to the creation of enlightened citizens. Any country is as good as its citizens. Their ethos, their values and their character will be reflected in the country's make-up. These are crucial factors that will determine whether the country will move forward on a progressive path or stagnate. Hence, there is a need to cultivate a sense of eternal values in each of its citizens, instil in him or her a sense of discipline. The education system right from the primary level has to concentrate on this aspect. For inculcating discipline among citizens, I visualise the necessity for providing compulsory NCC training for a minimum period of eighteen months to all our youth either during the senior secondary stage or during graduation in all educational institutions, both government and private.

All of us have to practise the values of honesty, sincerity and tolerance in our day-to-day living. This will elevate our politics to statesmanship. We have to collectively inculcate a positive attitude of what we can do for our country so that we together will be able to benefit ourselves. We have immensely benefited from what our ancestors did and left for us. We have a right and responsibility to leave a positive legacy to the posterity for which we all will be remembered.[15]

## Collective Effort

Once in a meeting with schoolchildren I asked them what they understood of the Developed India mission. A small boy replied through this story : Once there was a big forest fire in a jungle and all the animals and birds were frantically trying to escape. But one small bird rushed to the nearest waterhole and brought a beakful of water and dropped it on the fire. The fire laughed and said, "What a foolish thing to do instead of escaping the wrath of the fire." The bird replied, "Like me if all the birds and animals bring in water to pour over you, the entire ocean will be here and you will be put out in no time."

*We have a right and responsibility to leave a positive legacy to the posterity for which me all will be remembered*

As in the story, it is important for every individual to do his bit for making India a prosperous and developed nation. I liked the spirit of this boy and I am sure that, if the 540 million youth of our country work collectively, India will be a developed nation much before 2020.[16]

*Oh Almighty, create thoughts and actions*
*In the minds of the people of the nation*
*So that they live united.*
*Oh Almighty, bless the people*
*To take a path of life with righteousness*
*As righteousness gives the strength of character.*
*Help all religious leaders of the country to*
*Give strength to the people to combat*
*the divisive forces.*
*Guide the people to develop an attitude to appreciate*
*Different ideologies and transform enmity*
*Among individuals, organisations and nations*
*into friendliness and harmony.*
*Embed the thought*
*'Nation is bigger than the individual'*
*in the minds of the leaders and people.*
*Oh God, bless the people to work with perseverance*
*To transform the country into*
*A peaceful and prosperous nation*
*And promote world peace.*[17]

# ENLIGHTENED CITIZENSHIP

Enlightened citizenship has three components: education with value system, religion transforming into spiritual force, and creating economic prosperity through development[1]

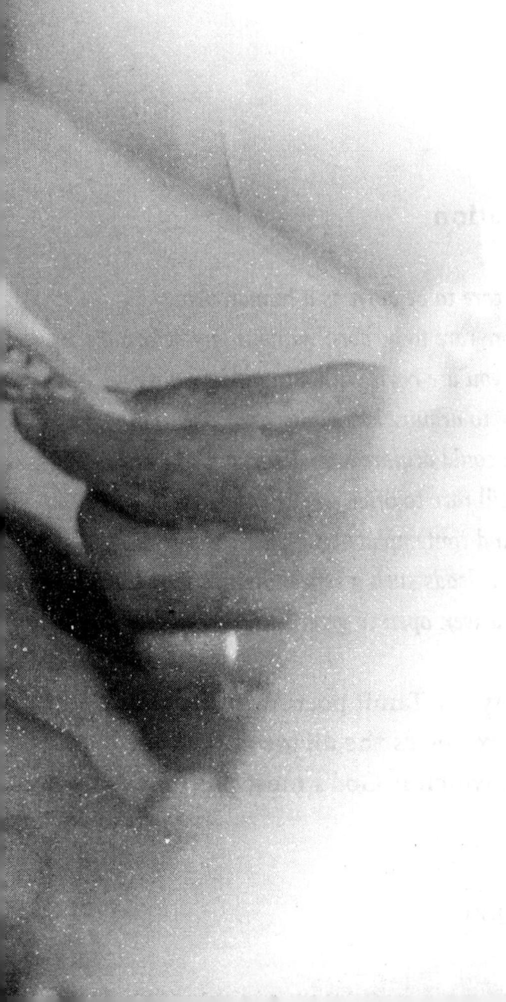

# ENLIGHTENED CITIZENSHIP

## God's Creation

*It is rare to be born as a human being*
*It is still more rare to be born without any deformity*
*Even if you are born without any deformity*
*It is rare to acquire knowledge and education*
*Even if one could acquire knowledge and education*
*It is still rare to offer service to mankind*
*And contemplate on higher self.*
*If one leads such a sefless divine life*
*The gates of heaven open to greet such an evolved soul.*

This poem by the Tamil poet Awaiyar beautifully expresses the divine nature of human life, which is God's most precious creation.[2]

For evolution of a prosperous, happy and peaceful society what we need is freedom from war—war within the mind and outside the mind—and above all a human heart capable of giving and empowering people. The road map for graduating into an enlightened citizen will have to include education with value system, religions graduating into spirituality and visionary policies graduating India into a developed nation.[3]

## Education with Value System

School provides the most important environment where the character gets shaped as children between the age of five to seventeen years spend almost 25,000 hours in school.

*Reverence for life is indeed possible if a philosophical thought of reverence can be transformed into actions by empowering the various components of society*

Ethics of giving to others should be cultivated by asking the questions, "How can my learning benefit others? How can I contribute to my own development and at the same time to the development of others and the nation?"

For imbibing moral development, values such as teamwork, fair play, cooperation, doing things right and doing the right thing, hard work and commitment to a cause larger than oneself are to be emphasised, while keeping in mind our cultural fabric and our own value systems.[4]

## Religion transforming into Spirituality

I was once invited by the Bishop of Rajkot, Rev. Father Gregory Karotemprel CMI to inaugurate the Christ College. Before the inauguration the Bishop invited me to his house. When I entered his house I felt as if I was entering a holy place. There was a unique prayer hall connecting all religions and respecting all religious sentiments. While the Bishop was explaining to me the significance of this prayer hall, there was a call from the nearby Swaminarayan temple requesting me to visit their temple. When I told Rev. Father Gregory of this, he said that he would also accompany me.

*All of us have to work hard and do everything possible to make our behaviour civilized to protect the rights of every individual*

It was noon when we reached the temple and that is the time it is normally closed, but that day it was kept open specially for us. We entered the inner sanctum of the temple and saw the deity of Lord Krishna placed in all its splendour. We all were received with the offering of *tilak* on our foreheads. It was a great sight with Rev. Father Gregory, Abdul Kalam and Y S Rajan all having the shining *tilak* on their foreheads. This incident demonstrates the strength of connectivity of different religions in our country leading to a unique spiritual experience.[5]

Every religion has two components : religious preaching and spiritual insights. The spiritual focus influenced by compassion and love must be merged as an integrated mission.[6]
The words of the Mother of Aurobindo Ashram provide us the direction for religion graduating into spirituality : "I belong to no

nation, no civilisation, no society, no race, but to the Divine. I obey no master, no ruler, no law, no social convention, but the Divine."[7]

## Economic Prosperity

As a nation we have committed ourselves to the goal of a Developed India by 2020. We need to achieve this goal by enacting appropriate policies and laws facilitating societal transformation. The core areas and programmes for development have been identified where integrated action would bring about development. Now implementation of these programmes in an integrated and, in a time-bound and cost-effective manner, along with providing the necessary services to the citizens equitably with ease is the challenge we have to accept and deliver.[8]

## Global Outlook for Universal Harmony

Every human being on this planet has a right to live with dignity; has a right to aspire for

distinction. Availability of a large number of opportunities to resort to by just and fair means in order to attain that dignity and distinction, is what democracy is all about. This is what our Constitution is all about. And this is what makes life wholesome and worth living in a true and vibrant democracy.

The increasing intolerance for the views of others and increasing contempt for the way of living of others or their religions or the expression of these differences through lawless violence against people cannot be justified in any context. All of us have to work hard and do everything possible to make our behaviour civilised to protect the rights of every individual. This is the very foundation of democratic values.[9]

## Dynamics of Warfare

It is evident that man lives on wars. We distinctly see that the pattern of warfare has three parts: up to 1920, 1920–1990, and post-1990. The first part was the human warfare period. The motivation for human warfare was either territorial greed or wealth or religious domination which in combination later led to the First World War in 1914.

The second period, 1920–1990, was a mechanised warfare period. During this period the world graduated to the use of new mechanised weapons and platforms such as battle tanks, fighter aircraft and submarines. The motivation was ideological conflicts between two societies, former Soviet Union on the one side and the USA and allied countries on the other side. The Second World War also witnessed disaster by the deployment of nuclear bombs on two cities of Japan. Also, it resulted in accumulation of 10,000 nuclear warheads by each side.

*Only when each and every citizen has been empowered so that he can lead a fulfilled life with dignity, will there be national peace and prosperity*

During the third period from 1990, it is economic warfare leading to globalisation. Supremacy of technology led to technology denials and control regimes separating the nations as 'developed', 'developing' and 'under-developed'. Now the world is facing a new kind of warfare, an integrated situation of religious conflicts, ideological differences and economic-market warfare. How do we combat these complex integrated phenomena of conventional warfare threat, cross-border terrorism, insurgency and threat of nuclear attacks?

## Reasons for Terrorism

Terrorism results from various factors such as differences in ideologies, religious fanaticism, discrimination and enmity between organisations and nations. Constant deprivation leads to frustration—frustration on provocation leads to alienation. Alienation can manifest itself in two forms—passivism and activism. Activism can manifest itself in constructive or destructive modes. Constructive mode leads to development; destructive mode leads to terrorism, violence and aggression. Certain nations have been indulging mercilessly in cross-border terrorism. We need to collectively address these sources of disturbance by formulating visionary policies for national development and by executing those mission projects with hard work and sweat.

At this point I would like to recall a poem written on a full moonlit night. There was a divine echo in the full moon night from my Creator. Shaken and bewildered, the echo engulfed me and my race :

*You the human race*
*is the best of my creation*
*You will live and live*
*You give and give*
*till you are united*
*In human happiness and pain.*
*My bliss will be born in you*
*Love is continuum*
*That is the mission of humanity.*[10]

## Enlightened Citizen-Centric Society

The United Nations was established in 1945 after the Second World War with the mission of bringing peace among nations and resolving conflicts as they arose so that war would not be waged between nation and

nation. What the world has witnessed today is that two major unilateral wars have taken place in spite of the United Nations. Hence, we need a world body which can facilitate peace, prosperity and knowledge among the nations, irrespective of the economic status of a particular nation. Indeed, the vision of the new world body has to be to facilitate the evolution of enlightened citizens on the planet.

## Our Challenges on Planet Earth

There are many challenges on our planet Earth of six billion people. There is shortage of water, increased atmospheric pollution leading to diseases, depletion of fossil materials and other natural resources, depletion of available land for agriculture and lack of availability of uniform opportunities to all citizens. Many nations are experiencing the problem of injected terrorism. The young people of the planet dream of living in a land of opportunity and happiness. We have also seen that the economic prosperity of a few nations alone has not brought lasting peace to the world. No single nation will be able to handle the situation by itself. Humanity will require mega missions for harnessing solar energy, providing drinking water from seawater through desalination process and bringing minerals from other planets. In such a situation, the present reasons for conflict between nations will become insignificant and unwarranted. India can play a major role in developing a new model of an enlightened citizen-centric society which will provide prosperity, peace and happiness to all the nations in the world.[11]

To the people who live a deprived life on this planet, I share a four-fold dream :

- A socio-economic movement based on technology and education that would achieve a secure and developed nation.
- Resurgence and liberation of the peoples of developing societies from an unjust economic order that is perpetuating poverty for the majority.
- Renaissance of traditions in the light of modern knowledge forming the outer basis of a fairer, brighter, and nobler life for all mankind.
- Unity of minds as a step in evolution towards the solution of the problems that have perplexed and vexed mankind in the 20th century.[12]

*The vision of a new world body has to be facilitating the evolution of enlightenzed citizens on the planet*

## The Lost Sheep

In the biblical story of the lost sheep, Jesus Christ asks, "If anyone of you has a hundred sheep and one of them gets lost, what will you do? Won't you leave the ninety-nine in the field and go and look for the lost sheep until you find it, and when you find it, you will be so glad that you will put it on your shoulder and carry it home. Then you will call in your friends and neighbours and say, let us have a feast, I have found my lost sheep."

As the lost sheep is of prime importance to the shepherd, the message for every citizen of our country from this story is that you may find around you a house which is not lit. Please help to light that house. Similarly, teachers in the classroom may find hundreds of bright students but a few may need knowledge with kindness. All teachers must locate such students and impart knowledge to them. Leaders of my nation, you may meet many people and help them, but you must look for those who need your utmost help and bring them to the mainstream. Those who deal with public administration, look for the last person to be serviced and make him or her feel that he or she is serviced with a kind heart. Similarly, the judiciary and law enforcement agencies should look for the marginalised persons, who cannot even reach you because of the multiple gates and layers between the judiciary and the citizen. The media as a partner in national development should celebrate the success of our people, whether it is in fishing, farming, craftsmanship or achievement of a rural area. The micro world of rural realities lives in the macro reality of a globally acclaimed India and the media has to capture this. Only when each and every citizen has been empowered so that he can lead a fulfilled life with dignity,

*I belong to no nation, no civilisation, no society, no race, but to the Divine. I obey no master, no ruler, no law, no social convention, but the Divine*

## Oath for Enlightened Citizenship

- I will love whatever profession I take up and I will try to excel in it.
- From now onwards I will teach at least 10 persons to read and write.
- I will plant ten saplings/trees and ensure their growth.
- I will go to the rural and urban areas to reform at least five persons from the habits of addiction and gambling.
- I will take responsibility for removing the pain of ailing persons.
- I will participate in the mission of realising the economic strength of India by combining it with education with a value system and by transforming religion into a spiritual force.
- I will not support any differentiation on account of community or language.
- I will lead an honest life free from all corruption and will set an example for others to adopt a transparent way of life.
- I will always be a friend of the mentally and physically challenged and I will work hard to make them feel normal.
- I will celebrate the success of my country and my people.[15]

will there be national and global peace and prosperity.[13]

## Empowerment

Reverence for life is indeed possible in the real sense if a philosophical thought of reverence can be transformed into action by empowering the various components of society. When a child is empowered by the parents at various phases of growth, the child gets transformed into a responsible citizen. When a teacher is empowered with knowledge and experience, good young human beings with value systems emerge. When an individual or a team is empowered with technology, transformation to higher potential for achievement is assured. When a leader of any village empowers his or her people, leaders are born who can change the nation in multiple areas. When religions are empowered and become spiritual forces, peace and happiness will blossom in people's heart. The medium for the transformation to a Developed India is the empowerment at various levels with power of knowledge of the enlightened citizens.[14]

# CREATIVE LEADERSHIP

Creative leadership is exercising the task to change the traditional role from commander to coach, from manager to mentor, from director to delegator and from one who demands respect to one who facilitates self-respect[1]

# CREATIVE LEADERSHIP

## Need for Leadership

What are those things that are necessary for building a Developed India? We have natural resources and we have human power. There are 700 million people below 35 years in the population of a billion people. What the nation needs is young leadership which can command the change for transformation of India into a developed nation.

Leaders are the creators of new organisations of excellence. Quality leaders are like magnets who attract the best people to build a team for an organisation, and provide inspiring leadership even during times of failure as they are not afraid of risks. A leader is one who thinks what he can give to others instead of asking what others can do for him.[2]

## Qualities of a Leader

In June 1983, when I was working with the Defence Research Design Laboratory (DRDL), the Integrated Guided Missile Development Programme was to be sanctioned and individual Project Directors for each of the missiles—Prithvi, Agni, Akash, Trishul and Nag had to be selected. There were many experienced scientists who were competing for these prestigious positions. Many of them were quite senior and over fifty years old.

To enable the selection of the most suitable candidate for heading these projects we followed a novel procedure. I called for a meeting of the Management Council of DRDL to finalise the criteria required for the selection of the Project Directors. I asked each member of the Management Council to go up to a blackboard put up for this very purpose and write one characteristic which he considered most essential for the Project Director.

*Quality leaders are like magnets, they attract the best people*

When all the members had written one characterstic each, the total list that emerged was :

- should be a postgraduate or have a doctorate in rocket technology or system engineering

- should have achieved excellence in any one of the technologies in missile area or in management
- should preferably be a good missile system designer
- should be a team person
- should be able to get along well with the team, and other agencies contributing to the programme
- should have minimum ten years of service left so that the Project Director can see that the missiles are developed and successfully lead them on to production stage
- should be a person of unimpeachable integrity.

When we discussed all the characteristics together, there was convergence among members that the credibility of the person in achieving excellence in one of the technologies or management was the first essential quality. The second required quality was that the selected Project Director should be young enough to design and develop the missiles and lead them to production. Third, the selected candidate should be a person of unimpeachable integrity. With these selection criteria, only those scientists in the age group of below forty years and who also satisfied the other two qualifying characteristics were kept in the selection pool for the selection of Project Director.[3]

I witnessed the blossoming of a young leader Miss Darshana Prakasam, whom I met at Rashtrapati Bhawan, a school student studying in the USA. Even though she is studying in the United States she is fluent and proficient in Tamil which is her mother tongue.

She is keen to take up a project to provide quality education to Indian rural children. She is confident of motivating other children to join her in this mission and mobilise funds required for this project. According to her, a leader should have fourteen traits of honesty, optimism, determination, looking beyond, judgment, problem solving, courage, being concise, collaboration, stimulation, providing assistance, fervour, public speaking and organisation.

*A leader is one who thinks what he can give to others instead of asking what others can do for him*

Darshana wants to be the coordinator of the children education programme and says she will decide what will be taught and how it should be taught. Apart from executing all important decisions of the programme she would like to oversee the teaching by the volunteers. She proposes to mobilise a number of volunteers with teaching ability to teach children both in the urban and rural areas. Once the children are taught she proposes to use the same children to educate other children in the village.

This programme will mainly be targeted at those children in small towns and villages who do not have access to learning leadership skills and are not in a position to exercise their maximum potential. Darshana feels that learning leadership skills is not as easy as learning arithmetic and literature. This is an example that many children can emulate and become leaders like Darshana Prakasam and create a number of similar enterprises.[4]

## A Leader Sees Far into the Future

*A leader gives the credit for success to those who worked for it and absorbs the failures*

In 1962 I was appointed as a rocket engineer in the Indian Space Research Organisation (ISRO), to experiment on payloads with various sounding rockets. One of the important projects assigned to me was preparing the pyro-jettisoning system of the nose-cone carrying X-ray payload for upper atmospheric studies being carried out. I had conducted several ground tests to prove the efficacy of the jettisoning system and was confident that it would work when I would be called upon to demonstrate the experiment to Prof. Vikram Sarabhai during one of his quarterly review visits. Prof. Vikram Sarabhai's coming was always a big event and everyone prepared experiments for it months in advance to prove their talent before him. I was getting ready with two payloads for the demonstration tests. Prof. Sarabhai came and the tests were carried out. To my great disappointment the first test failed. I checked and re-checked within the short time available to me, but the second test also failed. Prof. Vikram Sarabhai left the scene without saying a word. I was under terrific shock. I worked feverishly the whole night analysing the reasons for the failure and prepared a handwritten report. I realised it was a quality and reliability related problem.

The next morning I got a call to see Prof. Vikram Sarabhai. I was very nervous and was thinking that I would be required to explain the reasons for the failure. As I entered the room a warm smile from Prof. Sarabhai welcomed me and he gave me a paper approving a Rocket Integration Laboratory! That was the beginning of the System Integration Laboratory of the Launch Vehicle Programme.[5]

## A Leader Absorbs Failure

Two decades ago, while I was working at ISRO, I had the best possible education, the kind which cannot be provided by any university. I was given a task by Prof. Satish Dhawan to develop the first satellite launch vehicle SLV-3 to put the Rohini satellite into orbit. This was one of the largest high-technology space programmes undertaken in 1973. The entire space technology community was geared up for this task. Thousands of scientists, engineers and technicians worked round the clock, which resulted in the realisation of the first SLV-3 launch in the early hours of 10th August 1979. SLV-3 took off and the first stage worked beautifully. But the control system in the second stage malfunctioned and the mission could not achieve its objectives.

After the event there was a press conference at Sriharikota. Prof. Dhawan took me to the press conference. There he announced that he took full responsibility for not achieving the mission, even though I was the Project Director and the Mission Director!

When we re-launched SLV-3 on 18th July 1980, successfully injecting the Rohini satellite into the orbit, again there was a press conference and this time Prof. Dhawan put me in the front to share the success story with the press.

*If you aspire to achieve great things in life you need magnanimity*

What I learnt from this event was that a leader gives credit for the success to all those who work with him while he himself absorbs the failures. This is true leadership. The scientific community in India has had the good fortune to work with many such true leaders, resulting in so many great scientific accomplishments.[6]

## A Leader Celebrates others' Success

Prof. Norman Borlaug, a Nobel laureate and a well-known agricultural scientist, was bestowed with the Dr M S Swaminathan award for 2005. At a glittering function held at Vigyan Bhawan in New Delhi, he was in the midst of all the praise being showered on him from everybody gathered there.

When it was his turn to speak, he got up and highlighted India's advancement in agricultural science and production and said that the political visionary Sri C Subramaniam and agricultural scientist Dr M S Swaminathan were the prime architects of the first Green Revolution in India. He also recalled with pride Dr Verghese Kurien who ushered in the White Revolution in India. And then came the surprise!

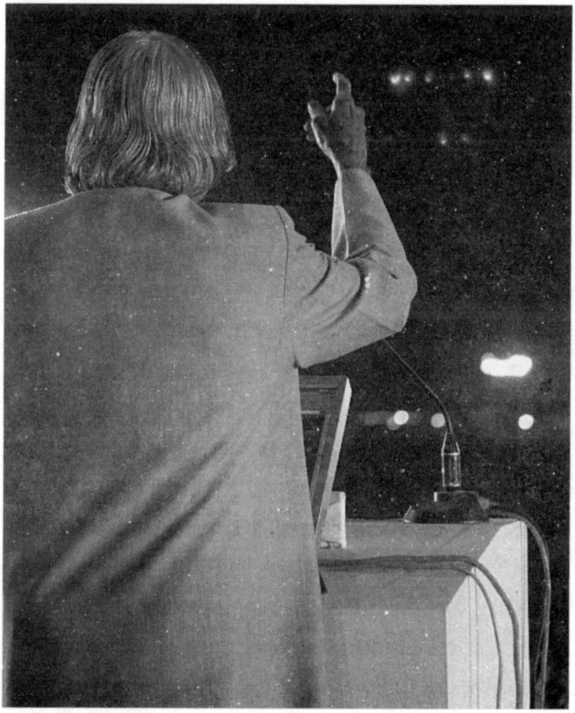

Dr Borlaug turned to the scientists sitting in the third, fifth and eighth rows of the audience and identified Dr Raja Ram a wheat specialist, Dr S K Vasal a maize specialist, and Dr B R Barwale a seed specialist. He said all these scientists had contributed to the Green Revolution and introduced them to the audience by asking them to stand and ensured that the audience cheered and greeted these three scientists with great enthusiasm. I have not witnessed such a scene on any other occasion in our country.

I call this action of Dr Norman Borlaug a scientific magnanimity and the mark of a true leader. If you aspire to achieve great things in life you need magnanimity.[7]

Recently I read a book in which it was described how the management of an organisation was able to retrieve a submarine it had lost in the ocean. When the management realised that they had lost a submarine, a meeting of four experts was called and several ideas were generated. But when a search was made using these ideas, no positive result was achieved.

Then the top management decided to call a meeting of all the forty people from the various disciplines within the organisation for working out a comprehensive search process. All the forty members were asked to give one mutually exclusive suggestion for progressing towards the search. The resultant forty suggestions threw up five alternatives. Based on these alternatives, five parallel teams were deployed to carry out the search process and finally the missing submarine was found.

This type of problem-solving technique is being followed in our Indian scientific institutions such as the ISRO and the DRDO, where programme review meetings are attended by specialists in multi-disciplines, leading to precise determination of problem areas and finding satisfactory solutions.[8]

*A great mind and a great heart go together*

## Moral Leadership

A leader provides moral leadership. Moral leadership involves two things. First, it requires the ability to have compelling and powerful dreams or visions of human betterment; a state of things in which human beings could be better off in the future than they are now. Second, moral leadership

requires a disposition to do the right things and influence others also to do the same.[9]

## Entrepreneurial Leadership

While moral leadership requires people to do the right things, entrepreneurial leadership requires people to acquire the habit of doing things right.

*The higher the proportion of creative leaders in a nation, higher the potential of success of visions like "Developed India"*

When I met Sabeer Bhatia, the entrepreneur of Hotmail fame, he provided some very interesting statistics. He mentioned that in the United States of America, 90 per cent of the wealth is generated by small enterprises which employ less than 50 persons in their establishments and the government encourages such institutions to grow. Entrepreneurial leadership has three parts to it. First, problem finding and problem solving in the context of development. Entrepreneurship starts with understanding our needs and realising that, as human beings, we all have similar needs. It begins with wanting to help others as we help ourselves. Second, the willingness to take risks. Entrepreneurship requires doing things differently, being bold in our thinking and this is always risky. You must learn how to calculate risks for the sake of larger gain. Third is the disposition to do things right.[10]

The key characteristics required in an entrepreneur are desire, drive, discipline and determination. Would-be entrepreneurs should have, and if they don't, they should inculcate, the following important traits :

- Have a vision and a pioneering spirit
- Be able to see possibilities where others do not
- Always search for new opportunities and challenges
- Be creative and 'able to think out-of-the-box'
- Constantly strive to do things better
- Be confident about taking risks
- Be proactive and focused on the future
- Have a good knowledge and skill base.[11]

*Enlightened leadership is all about empowerment*

## Leadership leads to Economic Development

There is a connectivity between development, economic prosperity, technology, production, productivity, employees' role and quality of management, all of which are linked to the creative leader.

> A nation's economic development is powered by competitiveness; competitiveness is powered by knowledge power.
>
> Technology and innovation are powered by resource investment; resource investment is powered by revenue and return on investment.

Revenue is powered by volume and repeat sales through customer loyalty; customer loyalty is powered by quality and value of products.

Quality and value of products are powered by employee productivity and innovation; Employee productivity is powered by employee loyalty, employee satisfaction and working environment.

Working environment is powered by management stewardship and sound project management; management stewardship is powered by creative leadership.[12]

*When a leader empowers the people, such leaders are created who can change the course of the nation itself*

## Creative Leadership

One of the very important ingredients for the success of the vision of transforming India into a developed nation by 2020 is the evolution of creative leaders.
Who is that creative leader? What are the qualities of a creative leader?

Creative leadership is exercising the task to change the traditional role from commander to coach, from manager to mentor, from director to delegator and from one who demands respect to one who facilitates self-respect.

The higher the proportion of creative leaders in a nation, the higher the potential of success of visions such as 'Developed India'.[13]

## Empowerment : the Goal of Leadership

What is needed is the evolution of enlightened and visionary leaders amongst us in all walks of life, whether it be politics, administration, religion, business, education or science, which has a bearing on the evolution of our nation and the society. And enlightened leadership is all about empowerment. It is thus the need of the hour to develop enlightened leadership amongst various sections of our society who

will have a vision for and a commitment to peace, progress and development.

When a leader of any institution empowers the people working with him, such leaders are created who can change the course of the nation itself. [14]

# INDOMITABLE SPIRIT

We need a spirit of victory, a spirit that will carry us to our rightful place under the sun, a spirit which will recognise that we, as inheritors of a proud civilisation, are entitled to a rightful place on this planet. If that indomitable spirit were to arise, nothing can hold us from achieving our rightful destiny[1]

PASS

# INDOMITABLE SPIRIT

## Courage to fight Disability

About one thousand differently challenged children who were taking part in the Abilympics were invited to visit Rashtrapati Bhawan. To them I recited a small poem which I had specially written for the occasion:

*We are all God's children*
*Our minds are stronger than diamond*
*We will win, win with our mighty will*
*God is with us who can be against !*

On hearing this a boy from Iran by the name of Mustafa came up to me. He had no legs and was fitted with artificial limbs. He thrust a paper in my hand on which he had written a beautiful poem in Persian titled 'Courage' :

*I don't have legs*
*My mind says: Don't weep*
*For, I need not bow*
*Even in front of a king.*

I was really moved by the positive thinking of that boy and his courage to face life with optimism.[2]

## Courage to Fight Injustice

During a visit to South Africa in 2004, I boarded a train at Penrich railway station near Durban for a journey to Pietermatrizburg, tracing the footsteps of Mahatma Gandhi. It was at this station that Mahatma Gandhi embarked on the fateful journey that in later years was regarded as having changed the course of his life.

He boarded the train on 7th June 1893 to travel to Pretoria, where he was due to meet his legal clients. A first-class seat was booked for him. The train reached Pietermatrizburg station at about 9 pm where a white passenger entered the compartment. Seeing that a coloured person was travelling in the same first class compartment he got furious. He immediately went out and returned with two officials who ordered Gandhi to move to the van compartment. When Gandhi refused and resisted, a constable pushed him out of

*A vision leading to higher goals of achievement is the first component of indomitable spirit*

the train and also threw his luggage out after him, and the train continued its journey without Gandhi.

*The second component of indomitable spirit is the ability to overcome all hurdles coming in the way of mission accomplishment*

Gandhi spent the night in the waiting room. It was winter and bitterly cold. Although his overcoat was in the luggage, Gandhi did not ask for it fearing further insults. Gandhi contemplated returning to India but decided that such a course would be cowardice. He vowed to stay on and fight the disease of racial prejudice. This event changed the course of Gandhiji's life and he said : "My active non-violence began from that date."

The train and the compartment in which we travelled were exactly similar to the compartment in which Mahatma Gandhi had travelled. When I got down at the Pietermatrizburg station, I saw the plaque in whose vicinity the Mahatma was thrown out. The plaque had the following inscription :

"In the vicinity of this plaque M K Gandhi was evicted from a first class compartment on the night of 7 June 1893. This incident changed the course of his life. He took up the fight against racial oppression. His active non-violence started from that date."[3]

## An Indomitable Spirit

I met Dr Nelson Mandela during my trip to South Africa. Dr Nelson Mandela is the person responsible for the freedom of South Africa. The two lessons one can learn from him are: indomitable spirit and virtue of forgiveness.

Cape Town in South Africa is famous for its Table Mountain which has three peaks, namely, Table Peak, Devil Peak and Fake Peak. Between the peaks it is a beautiful sight throughout the day, with dark clouds and sometimes white clouds embracing the peaks. Table Mountain is very close to the sea coast of the Atlantic Ocean. We travelled by helicopter from Cape Town to Robben Island. When we reached Robben Island, except for the sound of the roaring sea, the whole island was silent – the silence symbolising the thought that this is the place where the freedom of an individual was chained. We were received at the Island by Mr. Ahmed Kathrada, a South African, who was a co-prisoner of Dr Nelson Mandela. On the Island we were shown the room where Dr Nelson Mandela was kept during the twenty-six years of his imprisonment. What surprised me was that it was such a tiny room, where sleeping and all other human needs had to be fulfilled! It has to be remembered that Dr Nelson Mandela, who is six feet tall, was imprisoned in that tiny room for twenty-six years fighting against apartheid. The major part of his life was spent in this room on the island. He used to be taken for quarrying to the nearby mountain for a few hours in bright sunlight.

*Power comes from inside*

This was the time his eyesight got damaged. In spite of his body being tortured, he revealed to the world the indomitable spirit in him. During the years of his imprisonment he wrote a manuscript, in tiny, letters, working laboriously every night after the jail wardens went to sleep. This tiny, lettered manuscript finally became the famous book 'A Long Walk to Freedom.'

It was a great event for me to meet Dr Nelson Mandela in his house in Johannesburg. When I entered his house, I saw his three-dimensional form radiating with cheerfulness. I saw in him the mighty man who won freedom for South Africa from the tyranny of apartheid. I also saw in him a person who, when he became the President of South Africa, accepted as equal citizens people who had ill-treated him, practised apartheid and put him in jail. When I shook hands with him I felt that I was touching the hand of a Mighty Soul. A big lesson that we learn from Dr Nelson Mandela is explained in a 'Thirukkural' which means

that "for those who do ill to you, the best punishment is returning good to them."[4]

## What is Indomitable Spirit ?

Indomitable spirit has two components. The first component is that there must be a vision leading to higher goals of achievement. A couplet from the 'Thirukkural' by the poet saint Thiruvalluvar written 2200 year ago, expresses it thus :

வெள்ளத் தனைய மலர்நீட்டம் மாந்தர்தம்
உள்ளத் தனையது உயர்வு

That whatever may be the depth of the river or lake or pond, whatever may be the condition of the water, the lily flower always comes out and blossoms. Similarly, if there is a definite determination to achieve a goal, even against insurmountable problems, you will succeed.

The second component is the ability to overcome all hurdles coming in the way of mission accomplishment. Many of us who have gone through large programmes and projects would have experienced that success is not always in sight and there are many hurdles. The same poet reminds us at this point of time through another couplet that :

இடும்பைக்கு இடும்பை படுப்பர் இடும்பைக்கு
இடும்பை படாஅ தவர்

This means that a successful leader can never be defeated by problems. He overcomes the problems and becomes master of the situation. I consider that these two *kurals* characterise the indomitable spirit.[5]

## Power of the Mind

On a visit to Bulgaria I visited the National Art Gallery where I saw an exhibition of paintings mostly done by Bulgarian painters, including the birth anniversary exposition of the famous Bulgarian artist Zlatju Bojadjiev. I was very impressed and inspired seeing hundreds of his paintings, including those done using his left hand after his right hand had become paralysed. The indomitable spirit in him made him paint with his left hand. It struck me that constructive genius cannot be hampered by a physical defect, as the power comes from inside and motivates one to forge ahead with the mission of one's life.[6]

Perception of disability lies in the mind. A person with a pure and enlightened mind is a valuable citizen irrespective of whether he is physically disabled or not. The life of a differently challenged person can be enriched through creation of indomitable spirit in him.[7]

## What will You be Remembered For?

The two questions I often ask people I meet are :

*"What have you learnt so far in life?"*

*"What will you be remembered for?"*

Asha Ramaiah, an HIV/AIDS patient, who works as a National Advocacy Officer for the Indian Network for people with HIV/AIDS gave touching answers to both these questions.

> "True learning in my life began when it was discovered that I had HIV-AIDS and had to face the reality of my situation. My husband's family turned me away from their home and even my father told me to leave his house. My plight was like that of any other abandoned woman left to face life alone as a fallen leaf just drifting with the wind. At the first instance I had to face up to the challenge of mere existence itself. Thanks to the strength of my womanhood, I could absorb the feeling of shock, and overcome the trauma of being thrown out of my home. I realised that it was my responsibility to make efforts to bring about a change in the lives of other people affected with HIV/AIDS in India.
>
> Today because of my constant efforts and support from my fellow people living with HIV, I am not only accepted in my community but even people of high positions come to me for my opinion, guidance and counselling on various personal issues. My parents are proud that I have become a role model for others to follow. With family and a

*You will be remembered for creating that page in the history of the nation* good peer support, I got remarried to a person suffering from HIV. My husband encourages and supports me to work with my HIV fellow patients for betterment of our lives.

When we had to decide about having a child, I learnt how difficult it is to make decisions in the face of uncertainities; plunging into the unknown that may have the risk of having of a HIV positive child. We followed all medical guidelines to reduce the risk and came out victorious when, after waiting for years, it was confirmed that our child had no infection. Now we have the responsibility of planning the future of my child for the next twenty years. Our quality life time can be utilised for imparting our parental responsibility by ensuring him education, security and a future. We learnt that dreams do come true but only when you own them and accept the responsibility of the possible risk in pursuing them.

*You have to evolve yourself and shape your life*

I will be remembered by the people afflicted with HIV/AIDS living in various parts of the country and my family, relatives and associates for the courage I showed to stand up and face life, and for my efforts in sharing the light I have acquired in the midst of struggle."

We see how Asha, with courage, not only defeated the disease but more important how she withstood the onslaught of stigma hurled at her by her parents, husband and society This I call an indomitable spirit.[8]

What would you like to be remembered for? Would you like to be remembered for your Ph.D thesis? Would you like to be remembered for your innovative thinking? You have to evolve yourself and shape your life. You should write it on a page. That page may be a very important page in the book of human history. And you will be remembered for creating that one page in the history of the nation – whether that page is the page of invention, the page of innovation or the page of discovery or the page of fighting injustice.[9]

*Perception of disability lies in the mind*

## Awaken the Indomitable Spirit

"I would like to tell the young men and women before me not to lose hope and courage. Success can only come to you by courageous devotion to the task in front of you. I can assert without fear of contradiction that the quality of the Indian mind is equal to the quality of any Teutonic, Nordic or Anglo-Saxon mind. What we lack is perhaps courage, what we lack is perhaps the driving force which takes one anywhere. We have, I think, developed an inferiority complex. I think what is needed in India today is the destruction of that defeatist spirit."

These were the words of Sir C V Raman, the Nobel laureate scientist of India who, at the age of 82, was addressing a gathering of young graduates in 1969.[10]

How indomitable spirit gives the strength to succeed and transform the earth into a paradise of prosperity and peace is beautifully expressed in this poem of Gurudev Rabindranath Tagore :

*This is my prayer to thee, my lord – strike,*
*Strike at the root of penury in my heart.*
*Give me the strength*
*Lightly to bear my joys and sorrows.*
*Give me the strength*
*To make my love fruitful in service.*
*Give me the strength never to disown the poor*
*Or bend my knees before insolent might.*
*Give me the strength*
*To raise my head high above daily trifles.*
*And give me the strength*
*To surrender my strength to Thy will with love.*[11]

# REFERENCE

## Inspiring Lives

1. Address to the Nation on the eve of 57th Republic Day : 25.01.2006
2. Address and interaction with the girl children of the capital organised by the National Commission for Women, New Delhi : 17.01.2005
3. Address and interaction with faculty members and students of the Indian Institute of Science, Bangalore : 14.10.2004
4. AIR address on the eve of Children's Day : 13.11.2003
5. Interaction with students of Army Public School, Udhampur : 03.05.2004

## My Teachers

1. Interaction with teachers, Srinagar : 19.08.2004
2. Address to teachers at PGI Auditorium, Chandigarh : 04.09.2003
3. Address at the presentation of National Award to Teachers, New Delhi : 05.09.2004
4. Interaction with teachers at Bodh Gaya : 31.05.2003
5. Address at the presentation of National Award to Teachers, New Delhi : 05.09.2004
6. Address during the presentation of Awards to Outstanding Teachers, New Delhi : 05.09.2005
7. In response to a question asked during Address and Interaction at Visva Bharti University, Kolkata : 01.10.2004
8. Broadcast on AIR on the eve of Teacher's Day : 04.09.2003
9. Interaction with teachers, Srinagar : 19.08.2004
10. Broadcast on AIR on the eve of Teacher's Day : 04.09.2003
11. Address at the First Computer Literacy Excellence Awards for Schools, New Delhi : 29.08.2002
12. Address and interaction with students and teachers at Visva Bharti University Kolkata : 01.10.2004
13. Meeting with school teachers, Bhubaneswar : 14.05.2003
14. Address to the Nation on Teacher's Day, New Delhi : 05.09.2005
15. Address at the presentation of National Award to Teachers, New Delhi : 05.09.2004
16. Broadcast on AIR on the eve of Teacher's Day : 04.09.2003
17. Address at presentation of National Award to Teachers, New Delhi : 05.09.2004
18. Address at the Third Annual Computer Literacy Excellence Awards, New Delhi : 07.12.2005
19. Address at the First Computer Literacy Excellence Awards for Schools, New Delhi : 29.08.2002

20. Address at presentation of National Award to Teachers, New Delhi : 05.09.2004
21. Address at presentation of Awards to Outstanding Teachers, New Delhi : 05.09.2005
22. Address at presentation of National Award to Teachers, New Delhi : 05.09.2004

## The Mission of Education

1. Inauguration of National Youth Conference at Suttur, Mysore : 15.10.2004
2. Address at the Third Annual Computer Literacy Excellence Awards, New Delhi : 07.12.2005
3. Address at Governors' Conference, New Delhi : 14.06.2005
4. Address at the First Computer Literacy Excellence Awards for Schools, New Delhi : 29.08.2002
5. Interaction with students at Pondicherry : 01.11.2004
6. Address at Padma Sheshadari Bala Bhawan Senior Secondary School,Chennai : 01.12.2005
7. Address at the Platinum Jubilee of CBSE, New Delhi : 28.07.2004
8. Address to the Nation on Teacher's Day, New Delhi : 05.09.2005
9. Interaction with teachers, Srinagar : 19.08.2004
10. Address to the Nation on Teacher's Day, New Delhi : 05.09.2004
11. Interaction with teachers, Srinagar : 19.08.2004
12. Address to teachers, PGI Auditorium, Chandigarh : 04.09.2003
13. Convocation Speech at Jain Visva Bharati Institute, New Delhi : 20.10.2005
14. Address during meeting with his Holiness Acharya Mahapranaji, Adhyatam Sadhna Kendra, Mehrauli : 14.10.2005
15. Address at 'Career Fair 2004' Mumbai : 08.02.2004
16. Address on Teacher's Day, New Delhi : 05.09.2005
17. Address at presentation of National Award to Teachers, New Delhi : 05.09.2004

## Creativity and Innovation

1. Address at Veda Vyasa Vidyalam, Malaparamba, Kozhikode : 25.09.2003
2. Address at Children's Science Congress, Chandigarh : 05.01.2004
3. Address at the award function of Shankar's International Children's Competition, New Delhi : 22.03.2005
4. Interaction with College/University students at Peter Hoff, Himachal Pradesh : 23.12.2004
5. Address at the award function of Shankar's International Children's Competition, New Delhi : 22.03.2005

6. Address and interaction with students at JNRM Auditorium, Port Blair : 05.05.2005
7. Address at Bal Yoga Mitra Mandal, Munger : 14.02.2004
8. Address and interaction with students at JNRM Auditorium, Port Blair : 05.05.2005
9. Address at National Balshree Awards for 2002-2003, Rashtrapati Bhawan, New Delhi : 10.02.2004
10. Address at The Indian School, Dubai : 19.10.2003
11. Address at the presentation of 3rd Annual Award Distribution Function of National Innovation Foundation, Ahmedabad : 05.01.2005
12. Annual Lecture at Saurashtra University at Rajkot, Gujarat : 12.01.2006
13. Address at the presentation of 3rd Annual Award Distribution Function of National Innovation Foundation, Ahmedabad : 05.01.2005
14. Address at Visva Bharati University, Kolkata : 01.10.2004

## Art and Literature

1. Address at Prize distribution of Shankar's International Children's Competition, New Delhi : 17.01.2003
2. Address at the conferment of 38th Jnanpith Award for 2002, New Delhi : 27.09.2005
3. Address at 11th Delhi Book Fair, Pragati Maidan, New Delhi : 27.08.2005
4. At the presentation of 1,00,000th copy of 'Agni Siragural' at VC's Office Anna University, Chennai : 19.06.2003
5. Address at 11th Delhi Book Fair, Pragati Maidan, New Delhi : 27.08.2005
6. Address at the conferment of 38th Jnanpith Award for 2002, New Delhi : 27.09.2005
7. Address at 11th Delhi Book Fair, Pragati Maidan, New Delhi : 27.08.2005
8. Address at Sangeet Natak Akademy Awards, New Delhi : 26.08.2005
9. Address at the Centenary Celebrations of Bangalore Gayana Samaj, Bangalore : 20.08.2005
10. Address at Ramakrishna Vivekanand Mission, Kolkata: 21.01.2003
11. Address at the Centenary Celebrations of Bangalore Gayana Samaj, Bangalore : 20.08.2005
12. Address at the Diamond Jubilee Celebrations of Sri Rajarajeswari Bharatha Natya Mandir, Mumbai : 12.09.2005
13. Address at 52nd National Film Awards function, New Delhi : 02.10.2005
14. Address at exhibition of works of R.K. Laxman, Jaipur : 17.11.2005
15. Address at Visva Bharati University, Kolkata : 01.10.2004

16. Address at Prize distribution of Shankar's International Children's Competition, New Delhi : 17.01.2003

## Abiding Values

1. Address at Jawaharlal Nehru University, New Delhi : 12.01.2005
2. Address at Sri Satya Sai International Centre and School, New Delhi : 08.02.2003
3. Address at Indian High School, Dubai : 20.10.2003
4. Address at Regional Conference of the South Asian Chapters of Transparency International India, New Delhi : 25.11.2005
5. Address at the 15th National Jamboori of Bharat Scouts and Guides, Haridwar : 16.10.2005
6 Address at Regional Conference of the South Asian Chapters of Transparency International India, New Delhi : 25.11.2005
7. Address to the Nation on the eve of 57th Republic Day, New Delhi : 25.01.2006
8. Address at Regional Conference of the South Asian Chapters of Transparency International India, New Delhi : 25.11.2005
9. Address to the Nation on the eve of 57th Republic Day, New Delhi : 25.01.2006
10. A Thought on the Great Birthday, New Delhi : 4.07.2005 (Event)
11. Inaugural Address at the Convention on Evolution of a Good Human Being, Gurgaon : 19.04.2003
12. Address at Indian High School, Dubai : 20.10.2003
13. AIR Recording at the International Children Broadcasting Day : 11.12.2005
14. Address at inaguration of National Youth Conference at Suttur, Mysore :15.10.2004
15. Address to the Nation on the eve of the 57th Republic Day, New Delhi : 25.01.2006

## Science and Spirituality

1. Address at fourth Convocation of Jain Vishva Bharati Institute, New Delhi : 20.10.2005
2. Address at fourth Convocation of Jain Vishva Bharati Institute, New Delhi : 20.10.2005
3. Address at 12th National Children's Science Congress, Guwahati : 31.12.2004
4. Address to the Nation on Teacher's Day, New Delhi : 05.09.2005
5 Address at Bangali Engineering & Science University, Shibpur, Howrah, Kolkata : 13.07.2005
6. Address at the Golden Jubilee Celebrations of Jadavpur University, Kolkata : 13.07.2005
7. Address at Indian Physics Association, IIT, New Delhi : 31.03.2005

8. Address at First Computer Literacy Excellence Awards for Schools, New Delhi : 29.08.2002
9. Address at Bangali Engineering & Science University, Shibpur, Howrah, Kolkata : 13.07.2005
10. Inaugural Address at the Vivekanand Institute of Value Education and Culture, Porbandar : 12.01.2006
11. Address at Jawaharlal Nehru University, New Delhi : 12.01.2005
12. Address to students from various schools, Guwahati : 16.01.2003
13. Interaction with the students of National Institute of Technology, Srinagar : 19.08.2004
14. Message to students from Dayawati Modi Academy Schools : 20.07.2004
15 Address at the 125th birth anniversary celebrations of the Mother of Sri Aurobindo Bhavan, Kolkata : 27.02.200.
16. Address at inauguration of Spiritual Garden at Rashtrapati Bhavan, New Delhi : 26.06.2004

## Tomorrow's Citizens

1. Address at J.S.S. School, Suttur, Mysore : 27.12.2002
2. Address at 15th National Jamboori of Bharat Scouts and Guides, Haridwar : 16.10.2005
3. Address at Governors' Conference, Rashtrapati Bhawan, New Delhi : 14.06.2005
4. Address at inauguration of National Youth Conference, Suttur, Mysore : 15.10.2004
5. Interaction with college/university students at Peter Hoff, Himachal Pradesh : 23.12.2004
6. Address at Nandgaon village, Maharashtra : 15.10.2004
7. Address at Inauguration of National Youth Conference at Suttur, Mysore : 15.10.2004
8. Address at the First Child Educational Summit - 2002, New Delhi : 14.11.2002
9. Address at J.S.S. School, Suttur, Mysore : 27.12.2002
10. Interaction with students of Eicher School, Faridabad, at Rashtrapati Bhawan, New Delhi : 31.08.2005
11. Address at 12th National Children's Science Congress, Guwahati : 31.12.2004
12. Address at J.S.S. School, Suttur, Mysore : 27.12.2002
13. Address and Interaction with students, Tiruchirapalli : 20.12.2003
14. Address at Veda Vyasa Vidhalaya, Kozhikode : 25.09.2003
15. Address and Interaction with students of Padma Sheshadari Bala Bhawan Sr. Secondary School, Chennai : 01.12.2005
16. Address at Assumption of Office as President of India : 25.07.2002
17. Address and Interaction with students, Tiruchirapalli : 20.12.2003

18. Address at Assumption of Office as President of India : 25.07.2002

## Empowered Women

1. Address at Second National Conference for Women in Police, Mussoorie : 27.07.2005
2. Address at Second National Conference for Women in Police, Mussoorie : 27.07.2005
3. Address at Bishop Cotton Girls School, Bangalore : 05.11.2004
4. Address at Preet Mandir, (Home for destitute and abandoned children), Pune : 01.02.2005
5. Address at the General Assembly of Third World Organization for women in science and conference on impact of women's research in science and technology in the new millennium, Bangalore:21.11.2005
6. Address at RBVRR Women's College, Hyderabad : 05.08.2005
7. Address at the General Assembly of Third World Organization for women in science and conference on impact of women's research in science and technology in the new millennium, Bangalore : 21.11.2005
8. Address at Second National Conference for Women in Police, Mussoorie: 27.07.2005
9. Address at the Annual Function of Indian Women's Press Corps, New Delhi : 19.10.2005
10. Address at Second National Conference for Women in Police Force, Mussoorie : 27.07.2005
11. Address at RBVRR Women's College, Hyderabad : 05.08.2005

## Towards a Knowledge Society

1. Address at Doon School, Dehradun : 19.10.2002
2. Address at Indian Institute of Management, Kozhikode : 25.09.2003
3. Inaugural Address at International Conference on Digital Libraries - New Delhi : 24.02.2004
4. Address at Doon School, Dehradun : 19.10.2002
5. Address at Indo-US Million Book Digital Library Steering Committee Meeting (through video conferencing), New Delhi : 29.05.2005
6. Address at Inauguration of International Conference on Digital Libraries, New Delhi : 24.02.2004
7. Address at the launching of Digital Library of India Portal, Rashtrapati Bhavan, New Delhi : 0 8.09.2003
8. Address and interaction with the participants of the India Empowered Event, New Delhi : 20.12.2005

## Building a Developed India

1. Address at the inauguration of Bangalore International Centre, Bangalore : 21.11.2005
2. Address at the inauguration of 15th National Jamboori of Bharat Scouts and Guides, Haridwar : 16.10.2005
3. Address at the inauguration of Bangalore International Centre, Bangalore : 21.11.2005
4. Address at Children's Science Congress, Chandigarh : 5.01.2004
5. Address at Assumption of Office as President of India : 25.07.2002
6. Address at Children's Science Congress, Chandigarh : 5.01.2004
7. Interaction with students of National Institute of Technology, Srinagar : 19.08.2004
8. Address to students at Guwahati : 16.01.2003
9. Address at the inauguration of Bangalore International Centre, Bangalore : 21.11.2005
10. Address at the inauguration of Bangalore International Centre, Bangalore : 21.11.2005
11. Address on Assumption of Office as President of India : 25.07.2002
12. Inaugural Address at 200th session of Rajya Sabha, New Delhi : 11.12.2003
13. Address at Indian Institute of Management, Kozhikode : 25.09.2003
14. Interaction with the students of National Institute of Technology, Srinagar :19.08.2004
15. Address to the Nation on the eve of the 57th Republic Day 2006 : 25.1.2006
16. Address at the 12th National Children's Science Congress, Guwahti : 31.12.2004
17. Address at the 125th birth anniversary celebrations of the Mother of Sri Aurobindo Bhavan, Kolkata : 27.02.2004

## Enlightened Citizenship

1. Address at the Annual Lecture at Saurashtra University at Rajkot, Gujarat : 12.01.2006
2. Address at AL. Ameen Public School, Kochi : 26.05.2003
3. Address at Sri Satya Sai International Centre and School, New Delhi : 08.02.2003
4. Address at AL. Ameen Public School, Kochi : 26.05.2003
5. Address at opening ceremony of Swami Vivekanand's Ancestral House and Cultural Centre at Ramakrishna Mission, Kolkata : 01.10.2004
6. Address and interaction with students and teachers at Visva Bharati, Kolkata : 1.10.2004

7. Address at the 125th birth anniversary celebrations of the Mother of Sri Aurobindo Bhawan, Kolkata : 27.02.2004

8. Address at Inauguration of the Regional Conference of the South Asian Chapters of Transparency International India, New Delhi : 25.11.2005

9. Address at Sri Satya Sai International Centre and School, New Delhi : 08.02.2003

10. Address at the Convention on Evolution of a Good Human Being, Gurgaon : 19.04.2003

11. Address and Interaction with students and faculty of JNU, New Delhi : 12.01.2005

12. Address and Interaction with the students and teachers, Visva Bharati, Kolkata : 01.10.2004

13. Address to the Nation on the eve of 57th Republic Day 2006, New Delhi : 25.01.2006

14. Inaugural Address at Convention on Evolution of a Good Human Being, Gurgaon : 19.04.2003

15. Address to the students at the Satish Dhawan Sapce Centre, Sriharikota : 10.10.2003

## Creative Leadership

1. Address at Indian Institute of Management, Kozhikode : 25.09.2003

2. Address at Indian Institute of Management, Kozhikode: 25.09.2003

3. Address at Loyola Institute of Business Administration, Chennai : 1.12.2005

4. Address at Young Entrepreneur School of Tamil Nadu Chamber of Commerce & Industry, Madurai : 27.08.2004

5. Interaction with young engineers of VSCC, Thiruvananthapuram : 28.07.2005

6. Address at Kanchan Bagh K.V. School, Hyderabad : 19.01.2004

7. Address at the Golden Jubilee Celebrations of Jadavpur University, Kolkata : 13.07.2005

8. Address at Loyola Institute of Business Administration, Chennai : 1.12.2005

9. Address at S.S.N. College of Engineering Kalawakkam, Chennai : 17.12.2003

10. Address at Bhargava Auditorium, PGI, Chandigarh : 29.09.2003

11. Address at Young Entrepreneur School of Tamil Nadu Chamber of Commerce and Industry, Madurai : 27.08.2004

12. Address at National Convention of Small Entrepreneurs and presentation of National Awards, New Delhi : 28.10.2005

13. Address at Indian Institute of Management, Kozhikode : 25.09.2003

14. Address at Bangalore International Centre, Bangalore : 21.11.2005

## Indomitable Spirit

1. Address at Veda Vyasa Vidyalam, Malapramba, Kozhikode : 25.09.2003
2. Address at Sanjay School, Goa : 13.01.2004
3. Address in memory of Second Lieutenant Arun Khetrapal, New Delhi : 16.11.2005
4. Address at Bishop Cotton Girls School, Bangalore : 05.11.2004
5. Address at the Vivekanand Institute of Value Education and Culture, Porbandar : 12.01.2006
6. AIR address on Children's Day : 13.11.2003
7. Address at Sanjay School, Goa : 13.01.2004
8. Address during the inauguration of "A Conclave HIV/AIDS : A Uniformed Intervention" organised by Assam Rifles Wives Welfare Assocations, Shillong : 23.09.2005
9. Address and Interaction with faculty members and students of 11Sc, Bangalore : 14.10.2004
10. Address at Veda Vyasa Vidyalam, Malaparamba, Kozhikode : 25.09.2003
11. Address at Visva Bharati University, Kolkata : 1.10.2004